Contents

Introduction...

Understanding the Environment..

Within Iraq...3

Iraq and the West..5

The Insurgency...

The Enemy in Iraq...9

Fighting the Common Enemy..10

The Adaptive Enemy...11

Defeating the Insurgency...14

United States Strategy in Iraq..

National Strategy for Combating Terrorism..16

National Strategy for Victory in Iraq..19

Staying the Course..21

Addressing the Radical Islamic Ideology..23

Through Our Enemies' Eyes..28

Role of Islam..

The Basics of Islam..31

Diversity in Islam...32

Separation of Church..34

The Concept of Jihad..35

Islamist Ideology..

Stating the Radical Ideology..38

The Dangers of the Ideology..40

Ideology as the unifying agent 40

Legitimacy...42

Appeal of the Ideology 43

Declaring others illegitimate...45

Promoting the Ideology...46

Imams 46

Madrasas 47

An Updated Strategy..

Removing the Leadership and hardcore Insurgents 51

Engaging the Muslims 52

Silencing the advocates 58

Reducing the Potential Insurgents 60

Conclusion ....

List of Figures

Figure 1 - Illustrative Patterns in Targeting 12
Figure 2 - Average Daily Causalities: January 2004 - October 2005 13
Figure 3 - Operationalizing the US National Strategy...17
Figure 4 -Ideological Spectrum for Contemporary Islamic Views 54

Introduction

Following the impressive defeat of the Iraqi military forces in the spring of 2003, the United States now finds itself engaged in an insurgency that it neither anticipated nor prepared to fight. After three years of war, the conflict continues as the number of critics increases and the number supporters decreases.

Although the outcome of the war in Iraq is still undetermined, there is growing evidence to suggest that the current strategy and policies are not sufficient to achieve victory. To counter such claims, the administration refers to the election of government officials, the drafting of a constitution, and the establishment of a democratic form of government as positive signs that the United States is prevailing. Most politicians and critics accurately recognize that these signs are tenuous and fragile.

The issue at the center of most debates is the United States strategy in Iraq and its effectiveness. As one journalist has said, "After 2-1/2 years of halting progress, doubts are growing among military analysts and a more combative Congress that this is a winning strategy – or even a strategy at all."[1] Despite the growing criticism, the published United States strategy has remained constant. The three fundamental themes of this strategy are: 1) directly targeting of the insurgency leadership, 2) reducing the total numbers of the insurgents, and 3) absorbing the remaining members of the insurgency into the political process. The establishment of democracy and the revitalization of the Iraqi economy are the supporting efforts to these three primary objectives.

To win the war in Iraq the United States needs to expand its current strategy to include the ideological dimension of the war. To develop this new strategy, the U.S.

needs to understand how this radical ideology leverages Islam, and then we can effectively apply pressure from all sectors of national power. In addition to military power, this strategy should include diplomatic, informational, and economic power. To achieve victory in Iraq, the United States must develop and execute a strategy that defeats or neutralizes the radical Islamic ideology.

Understanding the Environment

The war in Iraq, like all insurgencies, is a complex, dynamic, and evolving phenomenon. The United States and its allies are currently fighting a war that is very different from the one envisioned prior to the U.S. led invasion. A wide spectrum of forces and influences are constantly at work within Iraq redefining the nature of the war. Politicians and pundits alike, continue to argue that the current situation is a direct result of previous mistakes, misjudgments, and oversights by the United States and its allies.[2]

Before analyzing the insurgency, it is necessary to understand the environment and influences that have produced the current situation. Iraq is a complex mosaic colored by history, politics, culture, society, and religion.[3] These dynamic forces interact and react in complex and sometimes chaotic ways, depending on where, when, and how these forces come together.

Within Iraq

Like all modern states, history shapes today's Iraqi culture, perceptions, and prejudices. Although, the modern nation of Iraq is relatively young, the land and its people go back as far as five thousand years to ancient Mesopotamia.

Despite its illustrious history, Iraq has never truly existed as a single unified country, except under oppression rule, either by foreigners or by Iraqis. "If one can speak of an Iraqi state, it is not yet possible to speak of an Iraqi nation. Iraq's present borders incorporate a diverse medley of peoples who have not yet been welded into a single political community with a common sense of identity. The process of integration and assimilation has gone on steadily since the inception of the (League of Nations) mandate, but it is by no means complete."[4]

Historically, Iraqi culture and society are the products of the tribal and nomadic traditions dating back to the "cradle of civilization." These tribal and societal allegiances and customs still prevail in Iraq, although their influence has diminished over time. At present, the tribal influences are strongest in the more rural regions and around historically tribal areas. The persistence of these tribal affiliations makes Iraq a geographic mosaic of allegiances and rivalries. The authors of "Assessing Iraq's Sunni Insurgency" state that the insurgency is most active in the places like Ramadi, Falluja and the Sunni Triangle where traditional tribal relationships and rivalries are deeply rooted.[5]

Like other societal forces, religion is also a complimenting and competing influence within Iraq. It is no surprise that most tribes also share the same religious affiliations. This overlap strengthens existing bonds and increases the tribe's access and influence to a wider portion of the population that shares these same religious viewpoints. Conversely, sectarian differences can widen and deepen existing divisions along tribal, ethnic, or political lines. Of significance in Iraq is the animosity and open strife between the minority Sunnis and majority Shias.[6] The Sunnis have ruled Iraq since the British first placed them in power in 1920.

Despite Islam's recognized status within Iraq, one must be careful not to exaggerate the extent to which Islam shapes Muslims' political identity. In a recent *Washington Quarterly* article, Daniel Brumberg states there are times and situations within modern Iraq where tribal and ethnic affiliations trump the influence of Islam. [7]

In contrast to Brumberg's claim, a recent *Washington Post* article suggests that the October 2005 election results were the result of religious loyalty and not political choice. According to one of the article's sources, "There are two types of authority: political and religious. And of the two, religious is higher." Other sources and interviews seemed to leave little doubt to the article authors "that the loyalties of the Iraqis lay with the country's clergy and not its politicians."[8]

Iraq and the West

According to noted author, John Esposito, Europe's "Age of Discovery," which began in the sixteenth century but came to fruition in the nineteenth and early twentieth centuries, continues to have a strong negative influence on both Iraqis and Arabs. Esposito, a recognized authority on Islam and editor of *The Oxford History of Islam*, states that Iraqis view their history during the late 19th and early 20th centuries as a period of humiliation, domination, and exploitation by the self-serving and self-centered imperialist European countries. "The emergence of the West (Great Britain, France, Spain, Russia, the Netherlands, Portugal, and Italy) as a dominant global power proved a military, political, economic, and ideological challenge to Hindu, Buddhist, and Muslim societies in Asia, Africa, and the Middle East."[9] Esposito continues to suggest that most Iraqis and others of the Middle East have not forgotten Europe's imperialism and exploitation of the Arab world. As such, it is probably not too far of a reach in the Muslim's world to refer to this period as the "Age of Subjugation" rather than the "Age of Discovery."[10]

The establishment of Iraq as a nation is, in fact, a direct result of Western involvement in the Middle East during and following World War I. The League of Nations mandate that followed the defeat of the Ottoman Empire produced the modern country of Iraq in 1920. In accordance with this mandate, Great Britain defined the territorial limits of the newly established Iraq, whose limits and boundaries suggested little regard for natural boundaries, existing traditional tribal areas, or ethnic settlements. The subsequent establishment of the Hashemite government, which the Iraqis viewed as illegitimate, led to 12 years of insurgent activity and internal conflict, with Iraq becoming a sovereign independent nation state in 1932.

Given this historical context, Iraqis are less than enthusiastic, if not pessimistic, concerning today's Western involvement in Iraq. To many Iraqis, this history is prescient and provides credence in their eyes that the current situation is just another attempt by the West to invade, subjugate, and exploit Iraq.

Steven Metz supports this evidence in his recent article, "Insurgency and Counter-insurgency in Iraq." He states, "The Arab world has little tolerance for outside occupation, particularly by non-Muslims, a tradition of violent opposition to occupiers exists. Long bloody wars were waged against the French occupation of Morocco and Algeria, the British occupation of Iraq, and the Israeli occupation of the West Bank and southern Lebanon."[11]

Finally, most Arab and even some European countries view the United States led invasion of Iraq in 2003 as an unprovoked attack against a sovereign nation. The Century Foundation publication, *Defeating the Jihadists – A Blueprint for Action*, states that "as a sin of commission, the Iraq War alienated crucial allies in the battle against jihadists, made friendly Muslims into skeptics, turned skeptics into radicals, and created a new battleground for itinerant jihadist insurgents."[12] This comment highlights the irony of the current situation. Iraq is now the very thing that the coalition went to war to prevent: a terrorist sanctuary with Al Qaeda and jihadist presence that far exceeds what was present under Saddam Hussein.[13]

The Insurgency

"Fundamentally the insurgency is about power: who had it, who has it now, and who will have it in the future. For major elements of the Sunni Arab insurgency it is about regaining power – as individuals, as members of the old regime, or as a community."[14] While this is a straightforward and accurate description of the Iraqi insurgency, it runs the risk of making the situation much simpler than it is.

The struggle in Iraq is multi-polar and has at least four major contestants at any one time; the United States and it allies, the Sunnis, the Shias, and the insurgents.[15] At the highest level, there is both internal and external disagreement between these stakeholders over the distribution, possession, and application of power, both for the present and for the future. Tribal, ethnic, and religious frictions further complicate these disagreements. According to Colonel Lang, U.S. Army, "What you have in Iraq are a number of different peoples, factions, ethnic and sectarian groupings of one kind or another all having been released from the coercion that had held them in a kind of stasis. The Iraqi people are now striving to achieve whatever it is they think is in their best interest."[16]

Lastly, one needs to recognize that the variously stated goals and interests of the various factions are often intentionally vague and obfuscate the real issues at hand. As Jason Burke, a respected author on terrorism and insurgencies, notes, "Their grievances are political but articulated in religious terms ...."[17] Burke's quote reinforces the primacy of religion and highlights how each group colors the situation and couches the issues in terms designed to garner them the most support possible.

The Enemy in Iraq

Today's enemy goes well beyond the Iraqi military and disgruntled Ba'ath party members loyal to Saddam Hussein and his government. While they are still present, these two groups are but a portion of the many loosely affiliated entities operating throughout Iraq against the coalition. One source claims, "The Iraq insurgency today comprises a shifting host of as many as 70 disparate groups."[18] If such estimates are accurate, the sheer number of groups leads one to assume that the current situation is not an insurgency, but rather a chaotic civil war between many factions with separate agendas and visions. In contrast to this expectation, the insurgency increasingly seems able to overcome the stated differences in beliefs and practices and operate at an amazingly high level of unity.

The enemy in Iraq is known and labeled by many different names: jihadists, foreign fighters, freedom fighters, extremists, terrorists, holy warriors, etc. To eliminate confusion, this paper collectively terms those individuals, groups, or organizations currently opposing the United States and National Iraqi forces as insurgents.[19] Webster's Dictionary defines an insurgent as "*a person who revolts against civil authority or an established government.*"[20]

The reality is that the Iraq insurgency is a dynamic movement, whose numbers and affiliations constantly change on a daily basis. The estimated number of insurgents varies greatly depending on when the estimate is given, who is included, and what, if any, significant events occurred prior to that determination. Beginning in the summer of 2003, the estimates were generally between 2,000 and 5,000. Since then, the numbers have increased with the most recent estimates somewhere between 12,000 and 20,000. [21]

In a recent CNN report, Henry Schuster reported that U.S. military sources estimate that

there are up to 200,000 insurgents in Iraq. This is an astonishingly high estimate vis-à-

vis the other officially published data. Schuster defends this information by stating, "The

sources say their 200,000 figure includes approximately 25,000 – 30,000 actual fighters,

while the rest are active and passive supporters, including fund-raisers, lookouts, and

even family members."[22]

Accepting the variances in both accuracy and methodology, a common trend

across all estimates is a sustained increase in the insurgency's numbers over time. This

continued increase in numbers, although episodic, shows that the insurgency is still

growing.

Additionally, one must realize that the insurgency expands and contracts

independently across various regions. This variance depends on individual or collective

opinions on how the potential insurgent(s) can benefit by supporting the insurgency at a

particular time. Illustratively, this means that while the insurgents' numbers in Najaf

may have decreased due to coalition activities, their numbers may have grown in Haditha

due to lack of sufficient Iraqi governance.

Fighting the Common Enemy

A recent study by the International Crisis Organization titled "In their Own

Words: Reading the Iraqi Insurgency," reports that despite the disparate numbers of

groups involved, the insurgency is better organized and coordinated than previously

thought. This reports claims, "(The insurgency) no longer is a scattered, erratic, chaotic phenomenon. Groups are well-organized, produce regular publications, react rapidly to political developments and appear surprisingly centralized."[23] Similarly, another report states that these disparate groups "draw considerable strength from political and religious ideologies, tribal notions of honor and revenge, and shared solidarities..."[24]

Mowaffak Rubaie, Iraq's National Security Advisor and former Shiite activist recently said, "there's no doubt" that once-nationalistic elements of the insurgency (are) drifting toward Zarqawi and his extremist Salafi sect...which seeks to establish a puritanical society modeled on early Islamic times."[25]

While these reports seem to agree on the increased cooperation and unity of effort between the various elements of the insurgency, at least in the short term; there is skepticism regarding agreement on any long-term objective. Referring again to the International Crisis Group's report, "To this day, the armed opposition's avowed objectives have thus been reduced to a primary, unifying goal: ridding Iraq of the foreign occupier. Beyond that, all is vague."[26]

The Adaptive Enemy

In *Iraq's Evolving Insurgency*, Dr. Anthony Cordesman, the Arleigh Burke Chair in Strategy at the Center for Strategic and International Studies, highlights the fact that not only is the United States facing a growing enemy, but also an enemy that learns and adapts. Rather than continue directly attacking United States forces, the insurgency has expanded its targets to include Iraqi police and military forces, and Iraqi civilians. As an example, Dr. Cordesman's statistics show that the insurgents are increasingly targeting "softer" civilian, religious, and government personnel. While the total number of attacks tripled during the observed period, the targeting of Iraqi forces increased five-fold and the targeting of civilians and civilian infrastructure by an entire order of magnitude. (See Figure 1).

DUE TO COPYRIGHT RESTRICTIONS
SOME OR ALL IMAGES ARE NOT INCLUDED

Figure 1 - Illustrative Patterns in Targeting

Another observation Dr. Cordesman recorded is the significant increase in daily civilian causalities. These statistics show that while the total number of victims slightly more than doubled, the number of civilians injured almost tripled over the same period and there were three times as many wounded civilians to coalition or Iraqi military casualties. As of October 2005, the daily average was 62 civilian casualties a day. (See Figure 2).

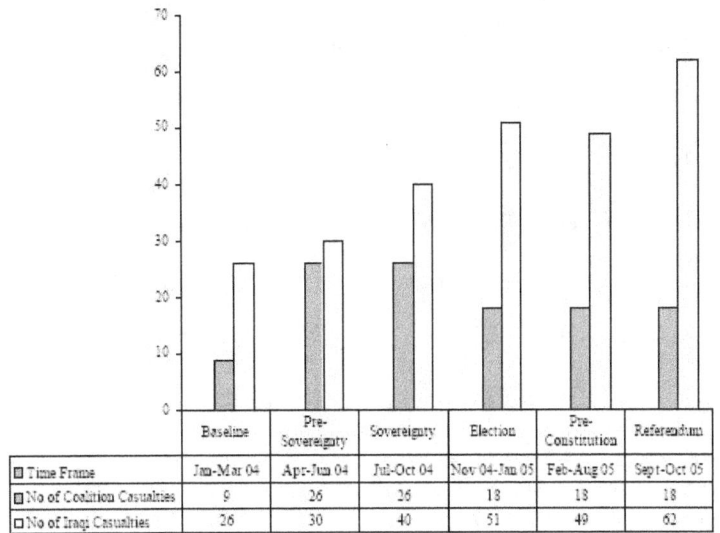

	Baseline	Pre-Sovereignty	Sovereignty	Election	Pre-Constitution	Referendum
☐ Time Frame	Jan-Mar 04	Apr-Jun 04	Jul-Oct 04	Nov 04-Jan 05	Feb-Aug 05	Sept-Oct 05
☐ No of Coalition Casualties	9	26	26	18	18	18
☐ No of Iraqi Casualties	26	30	40	51	49	62

Source: "Measuring Stability and Security in Iraq," Report to Congress, October 13, 2005, Page 24.

Figure 2 - Average Daily Causalities: January 2004 - October 2005

These statistics are important for several reasons. First, they demonstrate how vulnerable the Iraqi population is. By claiming these operations as successes, the insurgents are able to gain publicity, garner support, and recruit more volunteers. By exploiting this vulnerability, they are also able to use fear and intimidation to coerce unwilling Iraqi civilians to support the insurgency, either actively or passively.

Second, these numbers serve to discredit and destabilize the efforts of the United States, the coalition, the Iraqi security forces, and the newly elected Iraqi government. Cordesman concludes, "The insurgents conduct attacks of this nature to tie down manpower and equipment, disrupt operations, disrupt economic and aid activity and interact with attacks on Iraqi civilians and forces to limit political progress and help try to provoke a civil war."[27] The supporting logic is that if the United States and the Iraqi government cannot protect them, then perhaps the Iraqi people would be better off with a government created from within the insurgency.

Lastly and perhaps more importantly, the statistics reflects the acceptance of, or at least the preference for the tactics and methods as espoused by the more radical elements within the insurgency. The ideology of these elements condones the targeting of civilians and condemns anyone who openly opposes or fails to support their cause. While Cordesman states that it is too difficult to accurately define the insurgency because of its evolving nature, his statistics suggest the growing strength of the radical elements and their ideology within the larger insurgency.[28]

Defeating the Insurgency

The strategic significance and the increasing complexity of the situation make Iraq a particularly challenging problem for the United States. In order to achieve victory, the United States must consider and balance all of the various forces and influences present and then develop a stratagem that will produce the desired results, while simultaneously remaining acceptable to the major stakeholders. According to Ahmed Hashim, a professor of Strategic Studies at the US Naval War College, "With so many motives and goals, no single strategy will stabilize this situation, and a military situation alone will never work. Political and social strategies must be coordinated with military operations if Iraq is to achieve social order."[29] Hashim concludes by saying, "In order to develop an effective counter to the complex Iraqi situation, the American administration must rid itself of its pervasive arrogance and address its cultural ignorance."[30]

In his paper *Insurgency and Counterinsurgency in Iraq*, Bruce Hoffman, a noted insurgency and counterinsurgency specialist with the RAND Corporation, echoes the sentiments and concerns of Hashim. According to Hoffman, a successful counter-insurgency strategy must exploit the critical linkages between the political, social, and military forces at work. Based on his analysis of the counterinsurgency operations in Vietnam and El Salvador, Hoffman views the political/ military interface as the critical nexus of a counterinsurgency operation. Regarding level of effort and division of labor, he suggests, "90% percent of the counterinsurgency should be political, social, economic, and ideological, and only 10 percent military.[31] Both Hashim and Hoffman suggest that the United States strategy is too heavily dependant on the use of military power and does not put enough emphasis on the other elements of national power.

Finally, the establishment of some form of democratic government and its prerequisite stability is going to require significant Iraqi participation. This involvement must include leadership from all the major religious, tribal, and ethnic divisions within Iraq. Daniel Brumberg correctly assesses the situation in Iraq when he states, "As the drama in Iraq demonstrates, absent consensus over national identity, (the) solution requires a power-sharing arrangement that offer as many groups and voices as possible a seat at the table of multiparty government. This kind of consensus-building approach cannot succeed unless all groups check their religions at the door."[32] Brumberg obviously feels that overcoming religious differences is critical to the future success of Iraq.

United States Strategy in Iraq

National Strategy for Combating Terrorism

If we accept the United States' claim that the struggle in Iraq is the centerpiece in its "Global War on Terrorism," then it is appropriate that any discussion focused on the United States strategy in Iraq, include a broader discussion of the United States strategy in this "global war."

In the *National Strategy for Combating Terrorism*, President Bush clearly states, "The United States and its partners will ***defeat*** terrorist organizations of global reach by attacking their sanctuaries' leadership; command, control, and communications; material support; and finances." The strategy goes on to report that following this initial defeat of the terrorists, the U.S. will help states develop the military, law enforcement, political, and financial tools necessary to finish the task. [33]

The words "...the U.S. will help states develop ..." highlight a key contradiction in the United States strategy. Despite its stated goal of defeating the enemy, the United States strategy does not envision or intend to achieve this. Rather, it intends to sufficiently reduce or marginalize the enemy so that the host country government, whether newly established or long-standing, will be responsible for the continued suppression of the enemy's activity. "Operationalizing the Strategy" clearly depicts the continued existence of these enemy organizations, albeit with a "reduced capability," even after the United States has achieved the desired endstate. (See Figure 3).

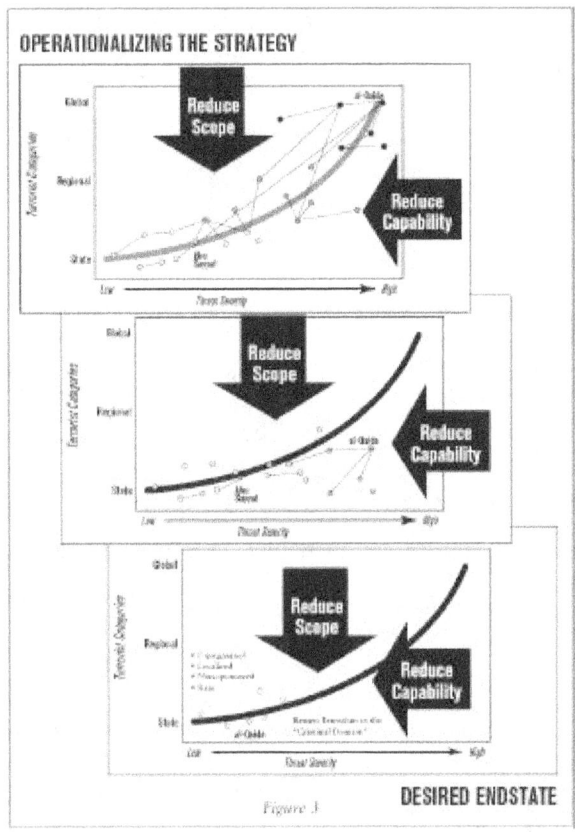

Figure 3 - Operationalizing the US National Strategy[34]

A series of exercises by the RAND Corporation highlighted this contradiction between the stated goals and the depicted endstate. Peter Wilson, a participant of these exercises who also serves as a senior RAND political scientist specializing in defense policy planning and research, expressed that "based on the exercise results, the current strategy does not put enough effort against the 'diminish' component, i.e., "diminish the underlying conditions that terrorists seek to exploit."[35]

Another exercise participant, Ambassador David Aaron, a career diplomat and currently a senior fellow and Assistant to the President for Research on Counterterrorism at the RAND Corporation, stated, "The National Strategy focuses on tactical steps and not enough on genuine strategy. For example, reducing terrorism to a local police matter is inadequate guidance for actually accomplishing the mission. It is not responsive to the long-term struggle inside Islam, which almost everyone saw as a crucial dimension…It is crucial to recognize that we are in an ideological war."[36]

While the *National Strategy for Combating Terrorism* acknowledges the ideological dimension, Ambassador Aaron's comments suggest that, in his opinion, the strategy does not adequately address the ideology involved.

Concerning the ideological war, the strategy states the United States must accomplish three goals: 1) de-legitimize terrorist activities, 2) engage moderate Muslim countries and governments to show the compatibility of American values and Islam to help reverse the spread of extremist ideology; and 3) find a solution to the Israeli-Palestinian Conflict. Moreover, according to this strategy, of these three tasks, resolution of the Israeli-Palestinian conflict is the one requirement "critical" to winning the war of ideas.[37]

The emphasis this strategy places on the Israel-Palestine conflict, leads one to believe its resolution will remove or significantly reduce the ideological friction between the Muslim and Western worlds. This is an idealistic, simplistic, and incorrect view of both the Muslim world and the issues it has with the West and the United States in particular. Resolution of the Israeli-Palestinian conflict will do precious little to alter the Muslim view of U.S. policies, that they fell are biased, applied inconsistently, and in some cases directly clash with traditional Islamic values, customs, and law.

National Strategy for Victory in Iraq

The *National Strategy for Victory in Iraq* is subordinate to the *National Strategy for Combating Terrorism* and articulates the President's broad strategy that drives the decisions and actions for the United States within Iraq. This strategy emphasizing the principles President Bush set forth in 2003, shows the strategic logic and linkages that connect the desired endstates, and then provides a synopsis of progress towards those endstates.

This strategy describes the enemy in Iraq is a combination of rejectionsists, Saddamists and former regime loyalists, and terrorists affiliated with, or inspired by Al Qaeda. While the accuracy of these descriptions is debatable, their presentation here serves only to demonstrate how United States Government views the enemy. Besides providing a definition and description of each group, the strategy also provides a National Security Council assessment of how to defeat each group. These descriptions and assessments are as follows:

- **Rejectionists** are the largest group. They are largely Sunni Arabs who have not embraced the shift from Saddam Hussein's Iraq to a democratically governed state. Not all Sunni Arabs fall into this category. But those that do are against a new Iraq in which they are no longer the privileged elite. Most of these rejectionists opposed the new constitution, but many in their ranks are recognizing that opting out of the democratic process has hurt their interests.

  ✓ *We judge that over time many in this group will increasingly support a democratic Iraq provided that the federal government protects minority rights and the legitimate interests of all communities.*

- **Saddamists and former regime loyalists** harbor dreams of reestablishing a Ba'athist dictatorship and have played a

lead role in fomenting wider sentiment against the Iraqi
government and the Coalition.

✓ *We judge that few from this group can be won over to
support a democratic Iraq, but that this group can be
marginalized to the point where it can and will be defeated
by Iraqi forces.*

- **Terrorists affiliated with or inspired by Al Qaida** make
up the smallest enemy group but are the most lethal and
pose the most immediate threat because **(1)** they are
responsible for the most dramatic atrocities, which kill the
most people and function as a recruiting tool for further
terrorism and **(2)** they espouse the extreme goals of Osama
Bin Laden – chaos in Iraq which will allow them to
establish a base for toppling Iraq's neighbors and launching
attacks outside the region and against the U.S. homeland.

✓ *The terrorists have identified Iraq as central to their
global aspirations. For that reason, terrorists and
extremists from all parts of the Middle East and North
Africa have found their way to Iraq and made common
cause with indigenous religious extremists and former
members of Saddam's regime. **This group cannot be won
over and must be defeated – killed or captured – through
sustained counterterrorism operations.***

- There are other elements that threaten the democratic
process in Iraq, including criminals and Shi'a religious
extremists, but we judge that such elements can be handled
by Iraqi forces alone and/or assimilated into the political
process in the short term.[38]

Finally, the strategy explains how the United States will employ national power

simultaneously along three broad tracks. The identified tracks are the political track, the

security track, and the economic track.[39] As written, successful implementation of the

strategy will create synergistic results across all three tracks. This translates to the

application of national power along one track reinforcing the efforts and successes along

the other tracks. These three tracks are the 'ways' the strategy will use to met the desired

endstates and achieve the ultimate objective of victory in Iraq. Based on these descriptions and assessments, in order to succeed, the United States must apply the appropriate pressure to have the 'rejectionist' accept and endorse democracy, marginalize the Saddamists, and physically target Al Qaeda cells and membership.

Staying the Course

President Bush and several other key government officials including Secretary of State Condoleezza Rice, Defense Secretary Donald Rumsfeld, and former Deputy Defense Secretary Paul Wolfowitz repeatedly stressed that the United States is winning the war in Iraq and that the Administration will "stay the course."[40] In a 5 October 2005 Congressional Research Service Report for Congress titled "Iraq: U.S. Regime Change efforts and post-Saddam Governance," Kenneth Katzman reports, "The Bush Administration maintains that holding to existing political and security transition plans, while working with foreign allies and pro-U.S. Iraqis, will lead to stability and democracy."[41]

The Bush administration has repeatedly pointed to the two national elections, the drafting of the Iraqi constitution, and its subsequent approval as irrefutable evidence to the efficacy of its strategy and policies in Iraq While they are indeed significant milestones, these victories appear hollow to a majority of Iraqis and Americans alike.

In spite of the Executive Branch's efforts to persuade Congress and the American public of the soundness the current strategy, significant criticism and doubt still exists. "In a 29 September 2005 congressional hearing, Rep. Ike Skelton (D) of Missouri asked General Casey: "What are we seeking to achieve? Are we fighting a counterinsurgency mission, or is our mission simply to train and equip Iraqis?"[42] Representative Skelton's comments suggest that he sees incongruence between ongoing military operations on the ground in Iraq and the achievement of the desired goals.

Other criticisms include a call from Representative John Murtha (D) from Pennsylvania, for a complete withdrawal of United States military presence by the summer of 2006.[43] Murtha's comments and recommendations make it apparent that he feels the United States presence is actually counterproductive to the ongoing effort within Iraq. According to Murtha, "I have concluded the presence of U.S. troops in Iraq is impeding this progress. Our troops have become a catalyst for violence. U.S. troops are the common enemy of the Sunnis, Saddamists, and the foreign jihadists." In response to several questions, Representative Murtha reiterated, "It's time to bring our troops home... They're (US troops) targets. They have become the enemy! ... We're uniting the enemy against us!"[44]

Murtha's conclusion is that any further U.S. military involvement is problematic. The perception is that any additional use of military force will only increase the strength and determination of the insurgency. From the Congressman's viewpoint, it seems that only the Iraqis have the ability to resolve the current situation and that the United States' role is now to provide political and economic support.

In contrast to Representative Murtha, Senator McCain, a Republican from Arizona, has proposed an increase in U.S. military presence in Iraq from approximately 150, 000 to 300,000.[45] McCain discounts Murtha's conclusions and suggests that the United States, its allies, and the Iraqi forces have not collectively possessed sufficient resources to apply the required military pressure to affect the outcome in a positive manner.

Lastly, there are those who state that the United States has made progress by gradually adopting or modifying the execution of its strategy and tactics in Iraq. In a 24 October 2005 *Newsweek* article titled "Finally, A Smart Strategy," Fareed Zakaria, a recognized expert in Middle Eastern affairs, stated the United States is finally progressing towards its goals, by adopting a more pragmatic and less idealistic strategy.

Zakaria contends that there are two major elements responsible for this recent progress. The first is the emergence of diplomatic primacy over military action. The article's author attributes this development largely to the efforts and insights of Zalmay Khalizad, the U.S. ambassador to Iraq. The second element is a shift in the military strategy "that defends towns and regions, thus securing people's lives, rather than simply killing bad guys."

Finally, Zakaria claims that although the U.S. tactics have shifted in the right direction, he acknowledges diplomats, politicians, and academicians generally recognize that the United States continues to place too much emphasis on its military power.[46]

Addressing the Radical Islamic Ideology

If we adopt Zakaria's position, that the United States' strategy is neither completely correct nor completely wrong, but rather needs refinement, then the logical conclusion is that something is missing from the United States' strategy. So, what is missing?

Since 11 September 2001 has proven to be the watershed event for the U.S. concerning its "Global War on Terror," the results of the 9/11 Commission's report may prove useful in answering this question. In its penultimate chapter, the report states, "The enemy is not just "terrorism," some generic evil. This vagueness blurs the strategy. The catastrophic threat at this moment in history is more specific. It is the threat posed by (radical Islamists) - especially the Al Qaeda network, its affiliates, and its ideology."[47]

In its report, the Commission recognized this radical ideology is significantly different from the traditional teachings and commonly accepted interpretations and practices of Islam. Additionally, the report states that these radicals are a political/religious phenomenon linked to the events that occurred within Islam during the 20th Century.[48] The Commission defines these radicals as an "Islamic militant, anti-democratic movement, bearing a holistic vision of Islam whose final aim is the restoration of the caliphate."[49]

While the Commission was careful not to name Islam as the enemy, the report clearly illustrated the logic the radicals use to pervert the teachings and practices of Islam in pursuit of their political/religious goals. One of the report's recommendations emphasized that the United States needed to do more than merely kill or capture the radicals. Rather, the United States must develop a long-range integrated strategy that not only attacks the enemy and his organizations, but one that also prevents the continued growth of this radical ideology.[50]

Although President Bush and administration officials have periodically referred to this radical ideology in speeches and interviews, no one from the administration has directly acknowledged that it is an essential component of the war in Iraq. Instead, "Western leaders such as George W. Bush and Tony Blair have reiterated time and again that the war against terrorism has nothing to do with Islam. It is a war against evil."[51]

President Bush's speech on 5 January 2005 clearly shows caution in its deliberate word choice to avoid misinterpretation and run the risk of inciting the Muslim community. On this occasion, at a town hall meeting in California, President Bush said, "... our war is not against Islam, or against the faith practiced by the Muslim people. Our War is a war against evil. This is clearly a case of good versus evil..." [52]

Shmeul Bar, a former Israeli Intelligence officer and a research fellow at the Institute for Policy and Strategy at the Interdisciplinary Center Herzliya in Israel, among others, argue that the President is merely exercising good political judgment regarding his selected use of Islam in his speeches and interviews. In a recent *Policy Review* article, Bar identifies the dilemma President Bush and others Western leaders face when discussing such ideology. By directly stating or even intimating that Islam is a critical element or catalyst in this struggle, the United States runs the danger of inciting further violence and potentially alienating a large portion of the Muslim world. As Bar accurately states, "An interpretation which places blame for terrorism on religious and cultural traits runs the risk of being branded as bigoted and Islamophobic." [53]

Taking a contrasting position, Paul Marshall, a prominent writer for the American Jewish League, suggests that rather than deliberately sidestepping the issue because of political sensitivities, the United States has avoided the ideological element because of arrogance and ignorance. Marshall states, "Despite repeated challenges to Western notions of law and political legitimacy, American policy-makers have shown remarkably little interest in (radical) Islamist ideology, and seem content to treat it as simple fanaticism. This is a disabling mistake, comparable to trying to fight Communism without bothering to learn about Marxism. If we are to defeat the jihadists and radical

Islam, especially on the battleground of ideas, it is imperative that we better understand their far-reaching ideological ambitions."[54]

If the United States' *National Strategy for Victory in Iraq* is correct and the United States can successfully marginalize the insurgency by improving the political and socio-economic landscape of Iraq, then one must conclude that the role of religion within the insurgency is a by-product of the political socio-economic factors. As a counter to this, Bar states, "to treat Islamic terrorism as the consequence of political and socioeconomic factors alone would not do justice to the significance of the religious culture in which this phenomenon is rooted and nurtured."[55] Finally, Bar argues that in order to develop an effective strategy to win this war, "It is necessary to understand the religious-ideological factors – which are deeply embedded in Islam."[56]

Given the sensitivity and deft handling of the role of Islam in their speeches and interviews, it seems that President Bush and others do recognize the importance of Islam within the context of the war, and as some suggest, they are unwilling to suffer the potential consequences associated with naming "radical Islam" as a central element in the conflict. Dr. David Little, Professor of the Practice in Religion, Ethnicity, and International Conflict at Harvard University, supported this position in a recent *Harvard Review* article. In "Phenomena of Faith – Religious Dimensions of Conflicts and Peace," Professor Little states, "I think that for the Bush Administration, the religious factor is undoubtedly important…To be sure, religion is not the only factor in the administration's war on terror. There are the obvious economic and geopolitical interests, which are quite independent of religion. Nevertheless, in Bush's mind, the religious factor is significant."[57]

A number of President Bush's speeches concerning Iraq and the larger "Global War on Terrorism" support Dr. Little's assertion. As an example, in his 6 October 2005 speech to the National Endowment for the Democracy, the President stated, "Whatever it's called, this ideology is very different from the religion of Islam. This form of radicalism exploits Islam to serve a violent political vision: the establishment, by terrorism and subversion and insurgency, of a totalitarian empire that denies all political and religious freedom."[58] The President then proceeded to liken this radical Islamic ideology to Communism and then detailed how, like Communism, the United States would defeat it.

Based on all of the preceding evidence, there are two possible positions concerning the ideological issue. The first position is that the current strategies are correct and that the radical Islamic ideology is not a critical element within the Iraqi insurgency. The second position, which this author supports, is that the Iraq insurgency is "religiously influenced" and that its ideological foundations are critical in determining the outcome of the conflict.[59]

Regardless of the reason, by failing to address this ideology, the United States unnecessarily puts itself at risk of losing the fight in Iraq and the larger "Global War on Terrorism." In his award-winning essay on strategy entitled, "The Global Insurgency within Islam," Grant Highland states, "Indeed, the politically motivated U.S. rhetoric to limit the conflict to a war against terrorism versus an ideological struggle of immense proportion not only limits the scope of the conflict, but also perhaps falsely constrains what might constitute victory in the future."[60]

Through Our Enemies' Eyes [61]

Viewing the war through our opponent's eyes is perhaps the best way to answer the question concerning the significance of Islam and any Islamic based ideology. In a recent *Parameters* article, Ralph Peters wrote, "We are not at war with Islam. But the most radical elements within the Muslim world are convinced that they are at war with us. Our fight is with the few, but our struggle must be with the many."[62] This comment emphasizes the reality of the situation. Regardless, how Western societies view the war in Iraq, the enemy's viewpoint is ultimately the one that matters.

In a February 2005, Christopher M. Blanchard, a Congressional Research Services analyst for Middle Eastern Affairs, presented a comprehensive document that reviewed and analyzed Al Qaeda statements and evolving ideology from 1996 through 2005. Blanchard chronicled how despite their lack of religious credentials Osama bin Laden and Abu Mus'ab Al-Zarqawi, the proclaimed leader of Al Qaeda in Iraq, have repeatedly issued fatwas, or religious edicts, and called for armed aggression against the United States in the name of Islam. Blanchard's analysis included the review and study of internet posting, videotapes, and press releases officially attributed to Al Qaeda leadership.

To illustrate his point, one of the media Blanchard cited was the October 2004 video tape in which Osama bin Laden welcomed and endorsed Zarqawi as Al Qaeda's leadership in Iraq. Beyond his recognition of Zarqawi, bin Laden identified the Iraq insurgency as "a golden and unique opportunity" for the radical Islamists to engage and defeat the United States in the global war "which the Crusader-Zionist coalition began against the Islamic nation."[63] Lastly, Blanchard commented that the statements by

Zarqawi and others displayed an uncompromising commitment to a consistent ideological agenda. Blanchard states "the political prescriptions outlined in the statements are rooted in an Islamic principle known as *tawhid*, or the principle of the absolute unity of God and an identification of Islam as an all encompassing religion, political, and social system."[64]

Other evidence suggests that this ideological view transcends the ranks of the insurgency from the top to the bottom. According to the International Crisis Group's report, "In Their Own Words: Reading the Iraqi Insurgency," "Even at an early stage, when foreign fighters in all likelihood played a negligible part in day-to-day operations, the upsurge in attacks during the month of Ramadan in 2003, illustrates the extent to which the struggle was framed as a religious duty."[65]

Tracing the insurgency's evolution, the International Crisis Group study revealed several trends. First, was that the radicals have gradually come to dominate the actions and policies of the insurgency. Second, was that many of the insurgency's disparate groups, who lacked legitimacy and feared internal conflict, "converged around Islamic discourse, turning principally to *salafi ulama*, religious scholars, for moral and juridical validation. By doing this, the insurgents solicited the views of prestigious religious jurists who openly sanctioned their struggle." The final trend was that the more active elements or groups within the insurgency used Koranic passages and referred to the current events of Iraq in terms of the Crusades. The use of these passages and references seeks to invoke visions of earlier religious events and people such as the battle of Hittin in the early age of Islam; the heroic figures of Saladin, liberator of Jerusalem, and al-Qa'qa'; the early Muslim fighters, etc.[66]

It is important to point out that the increased use of Islamic terms and themes should not suggest that all of the insurgency's disparate groups have come to consensus on their goals. Instead, this increased use only signifies that these groups have leveraged Islam to maintain strength and to gain unity of effort in pursuit of their goals. A recent study by the Washington Institute for Near East Policy states, "The insurgents travel along parallel, often mutually supportive paths – sometimes acting alone, sometimes working together – in the pursuit of a series of common objectives that they believe will help them achieve their divergent strategic goals."[67]

In his recent article, "Terror in the Name of God," Mark Juergensmeyer, a professor of sociology and the director of international studies at University of California at Santa Barbara, writes, "One cannot deny that the ideals and ideas of these vicious (insurgents) are permeated with religion."[68] He continues to say that, this religious context allows the insurgents to employ violence within the image of a larger spiritual struggle that exists within every religion: the classic battle of "good versus evil." Juergensmeyer recognizes that the insurgents have made this a war of "religious influence" by framing their goals, grievances, and justification in Islamic terms.[69]

The tying of political objectives to the beliefs and teachings of Islam has created a loyalty amongst fellow Muslims and a direct linkage or identity with certain Islamic sects. It is this loyalty and identity within the Muslim world that we have failed to either recognize or have just ignored. "Most Americans – experts, officials, and civilians – have still not addressed the role of Islam within the context of the war in a frank and analytic manner."[70]

Role of Islam

While terrorism – even in the form of suicide attacks – is not an Islamic phenomenon by definition, it cannot be ignored that the lion's share of terrorist acts and the most devastating of them in recent years have been perpetrated in the name of Islam. This fact has sparked a fundamental debate both in the West and within the Muslim world regarding the link between these acts and the teachings of Islam. [71]

Shmeul Bar,
The Religious Sources of Islamic Terrorism

As the above quote suggests, if there is a linkage between the Iraqi insurgency and Islam, then it is imperative to establish a fundamental understanding of Islam. This understanding will serve as a common frame of reference, which will enable us to explore the ideology as it supports the Iraqi insurgency.

The Basics of Islam

Islam, the proper name for the religion, is "derived from the (Arabic) root *s-l-m*, which means primarily "peace" but in a secondary sense "surrender." Its full connotation is "the peace that comes when one's life is surrendered to God." [72] Muslim is the proper title for a follower of Islam. Like Judaism and Christianity, Islam is both a Semitic and a monotheistic religion. [73] Although all three religions share commonalities, each faith supports different beliefs concerning the prophets of God and of God's revelation to man.

The practices of faith as reveled and executed by Muhammad serve as the basis for modern Islam. The Koran and the hadith are the two principal resources governing the actual practice of faith. The Koran, similar to the Christian Bible or the Jewish Torah, is the Muslim holy book and contains the scriptures and revelations of God as Muhammad witnessed them. The hadith, which are recorded stories and anecdotes of the traditions of the faith that Muhammad practiced, serve as historical precedents to guide the faithful in situations not prescribed or encountered in the Koran.

Islam centers on five main pillars or tenets. The first pillar is the confession of faith, or *Shahadah*. The second pillar is the obligation to prayer. The practice of Islam requires Muslim to pray five times daily with certain allowances and exceptions according to traditions. The third pillar is almsgiving, or charity. It is an obligation of faith for every Muslim to donate to charity for the less fortunate. The fourth pillar is fasting during the observance of Ramadan, Islam's holy month. For the entire month of Ramadan, Muslims refrain from food, drink, and smoking each day from sunrise to sunset. The fifth and final pillar of Islam is pilgrimage. At least once during their life, if they are physically and financially able, each Muslim will make the pilgrimage from Medina to Mecca. The pilgrimage symbolizes and honors the climatic revelation of God to Muhammad.

Diversity in Islam

The modern practices and beliefs of Islam cover a wide spectrum from fundamentalism to secularism. One reason for the wide range of practices within Islam is the lack of a recognized central governing body. Comparing it to the Catholic Church, Islam does not have an equivalent to either the Pope or the Vatican. Instead, Islam relies on its hierarchy of religious elders, clerics, imams, and Ayatollahs in addition to its ulamma, or religious scholars. These religious leaders are responsible for providing guidance and making decisions in accordance with their perception of Islam. This lack of centralization grants these religious leaders an extraordinary amount of authority and discretion. This is especially true concerning their interpretation of the Koran and hadith. As it can be with any translation, modern interpretations of the Koran and hadith are susceptible to subjectivity based on the influences and factors present at both the time of writing and at the time of translation.

The two primary sects of Islam are Sunni and Shia. The former comprise approximately 85% of today's global Muslim population and the latter make up the remaining 15%.[74] Their divergence in the understanding, belief, and practice of Islam dates back to the death of Muhammad. According to the *Oxford History of Islam*, the concern over the political and religious leadership after the death of Muhammad caused this division. The first and most basic challenge the followers of Muhammad faced following his death was whether they were to form a single polity or were they to remain as separate communities, each headed by its own political leader. These original followers chose to unite and Abu Bakr, became Muhammad's first successor. Islamic tradition refers to Abu Bakr and subsequent leaders of the Islamic community as caliphs. This term comes from the Arabic word *khalifa*, meaning "successor" or "representative."[75] However, this unity was short lived when the 4th caliph, Ali ibn Abi Talib, Muhammad's cousin and direct blood relation, was assassinated in 661 AD. As result of this assassination, the faith divided into the two groups that we now recognize as the Sunnis and Shias.

Sunnis believe that the selected leader, or caliph, serves as the protector of the faith and but does not enjoy any special religious status or inspiration. This and other related beliefs of the Sunnis essentially establishes a division of labor, responsibilities, and power between the caliph and the senior religious leaders. Shias, by contrast, believe that succession to the leadership of the Muslim community is hereditary and the caliph should serve as both a political and religious leader.[76] This division and its corresponding sectarian allegiances serve as a major political fissure within Iraq.

P.J. Vatikiotis, a Professor of Middle East Politics at the University of London, attributes the variances of Islamic practices to the societal environment in which these variances occur. According to Vatikiotis,

> "There is not simply intellectual but also wider disagreement among Muslims over what Islam is. Although Muslims share one faith and a common Islamic sentiment, the social structures in which these prevail differ from one Islamic society or country to another. Historically and in practice, there has been no single or uniform Islamic experience or understanding of Islam.... This was as true in its classical and medieval period as it has been in its modern age. It is not surprising then that there is disagreement among Muslims today over what is Islam, since its reality differs from one Muslim community to the other."[77]

Separation of Church and State

As with the other aspects of Islam, there is no single answer concerning the separation of church and state. According to Esposito, in *What Everyone Needs to Know about Islam*, "Muslims believe that their primary act of faith is to strive to implement God's will in both their private and their public life. Throughout history, being a Muslim has meant not only belonging to a religious community of fellow believers but also living in an Islamic state governed by Islamic law (in theory not always in practice)."[78] Additionally Esposito says, "Many Muslims describe Islam as a "total way of life." They believe that religion cannot be separated from social and political life, since religion informs every action that a person takes."[79]

To counter this, Daniel Brumberg, an associate professor of government at

Georgetown University, states, "… many Muslims, both practicing and non-practicing,

believe that their version of Islam should be separated or at least distanced from politics.

Indeed, little consensus exists in the Arab world about the proper relationship between

mosque and state."[80]

This contradiction of views regarding the relationship between religion and the

state seems to present an accurate portrayal of the variances within the global Islamic

community. The wide divergence in relationships between Islam and the state in Muslim

nations of the Middle East, Indonesia, and North Africa seems to bear this reality out.

The Concept of Jihad

"Jihad is a concept with multiple meanings, used and abused throughout Islamic

history."[81] The term "jihad" has become almost universally recognized and synonymous

with a "holy war" or a crusade. In actuality, the Arabic word *jihad* (verbal noun of the

verb jahada) means to strive, to exert oneself, to struggle. The word has a basic

connotation of an endeavor towards a praiseworthy aim. [82] Muslims commonly refer to

two forms of jihad; the greater jihad and the lesser jihad. The greater jihad is also called

the "jihad of the pen" and the lesser jihad as the "jihad of the sword."

Esposito, in *What Everyone needs to know about Islam*, writes, "In its most

general meaning, jihad refers to the obligation incumbent on all Muslims, individuals and

the community, to follow and realize God's will: to lead a virtuous life and to extend the

Islamic community through preaching, education, example, writing, etc. Efforts along

this line are recognized forms of the greater jihad."[83]

Ruldoph Peters, author of *Jihad: in Classical and Modern Islam*, describes the greater jihad as follows: "In a religious context it may express a struggle against one's evil inclinations or an exertion for the sake of Islam and the ummah."[84] Most texts use similar terms to describe the greater jihad. Examples include efforts trying to convert non-believers to Islam, trying to improve one's own practice of Islam, and working for the moral betterment of the Islamic society. Other names for the greater jihad include "jihad of the tongue" and "jihad of the pen."

In contrast to the peaceful means employed in the greater jihad, the lesser jihad advocates the armed struggle against the non-believers. The original intent and purpose of the lesser jihad was to ensure the right, in fact, the obligation for Muslims to defend Islam and the community of the faithful from aggression."[85]

The Koranic depictions of an armed struggle under the concept of the jihad go back to the wars the Prophet Muhammad fought. This form of jihad is the result of several forces. First, Islamic law forbids Muslims from waging war amongst fellow Muslims. The intent of this early Islamic law was to quell the violence amongst the early Islamic tribes and communities. As a result, in order for a Muslim to go to battle, he must fight a non-believer or non-Muslim.

Second, the early Muslims were subject to raiding and open warfare and as such, the concept of jihad obligated all Muslims to defend their fellow Muslims and Islam. Again, according to Peters, the precedent of Muhammad fighting the unbelievers survives and serves as the foundation of today's modern jihad, an armed struggle against the unbelievers.[86]

A relatively recent variation to the concept of jihad is it is a universal calling. According to this concept, the call for jihad obligates all Muslims, regardless of where they are physically in relation to the conflict, to support the jihad. Muslims can support this obligation either directly of indirectly. Indirect methods of support include recruitment, donation or procurement of equipment and supplies, and financial backing. Another prevalent position regarding this new universal nature of jihad is the authorization and encouragement of all Muslims to engage in jihad on a global scale against all non-believers until Islam is victorious.[87] Bin Laden, Zarqawi, and others routinely encourage such universal operations in their publicized statements and edicts.[88]

Finally, Esposito describes how modern groups take the historical teachings and precedent of jihad and manipulate the term and the context of jihad to meet their own needs and requirements. "A radical violent minority combine militancy with messianic visions to inspire and mobilize an army of God whose jihad they believe will liberate Muslims at home and abroad. Despite the fact that the jihad is not supposed to be used for aggressive warfare, it has been and continues to be so used by rulers, governments, and individuals…."[89]

Islamist Ideology

The use or abuse of religious ideology in pursuit of one's military or political goals is not a new phenomenon. "Throughout history, the sacred scriptures of Judaism, Christianity, and Islam have been used and abused, interpreted and misinterpreted, to justify resistance and liberation struggles, extremism and terrorism, holy and unholy wars."[90] "What these formulations have in common is the idea of a transcendent cause which may be employed to justify nearly anything."[91]

While the strength and unity of purpose that religious ideology provides is not measurable, it should not mean that one should overlook or underestimate its potential. In a 6 February 2006 article entitled "The Counterrevolution in Military Affairs," Ralph Peters emphasizes the importance of ideology as an element of warfare.

> "Faith is the great strategic factor that unbelieving faculties and bureaucracies ignore. It may be the crucial issue of this century. And we cannot even speak about it honestly. Give me a warrior drunk with faith, and I will show you a weapon beyond the dreams of any laboratory. Our guided bombs may kill individual terrorists, but the terrorists know that our weapons can't kill his God."[92]

Stating the Radical Ideology

Most experts agree that the radical ideology present within the Iraqi insurgency is a variation of either Wahabbism or Salafism. Both ideologies are very conservative in their interpretations of Islam and advocate the rigid observance of their particular Islamic traditions and customs. The basic logic that supports and perpetuates such ideology is the notion that Islam is the answer to people's problems. These problems include poverty, unemployment, lack of education, loss of social standing, etc. As the belief goes, by being a better Muslim and by strictly observing the practices and beliefs of Islam, God will recognize this obedience and reward these faithful followers.

Only three major groups within the Iraq insurgency , the Tandhim al-Qa'ida Bilad al-Rafidayan, Jaysh Ansar al-Sunna, and Al-Jaysh al-Islami fil-'Iraq, proclaim to be followers of such ideology.[93] Some sources estimate these groups only make up about 10-20 percent of the insurgency's total strength, but despite their limited numbers, they are among the most powerful in terms of their actions, their resources, and their influence. One source states, "These (radicals) do not interpret Islam in terms of dominant Western values – at least not explicitly. Rather, they have sought to assert Islam's domination, to interpret modernity according to Islamic values…"[94] According to former CIA analyst and researcher Marc Sageman, these radical Islamists advocate a strict interpretation of the Koran and their stated goal is to "reinstate the fallen Caliphate and regain its lost glory."[95] Sageman continues to say these radicals believe that because modern-day Muslim leaders "refuse to impose sharia, the strict Koranic law and true Islamic way of life … (they) are accused of apostasy and deserve death."[96]

To help complete the picture of this ideology John Esposito writes, "(Radical) Islamists continue to support the notion of membership in the ummah (the community of the Islam) as the primary identity for all Muslims, rather than ethnic, linguistic, or geographical identities. Contemporary Muslims still believe in the ummah as a social identity, despite the secularization of public life and contemporary emphasis on national political identities."[97]

A recent declaration by Mus'ab al-Zarqawi's legal council supports this concept of the ummah. In the 20 October 2005 statement to the Islamic Revival Organization,

Zarqawi's legal council defined the ummah as follows: "No matter who a person is, even if they are Iraqis … so whoever disregards his religion and abandons the Muslim populace, their blood should be spilled. There is no difference between an Iraqi and a non-Iraqi." The statement finished by saying, "If an American Muslim, who believes in all that Islam holds and denounces tyranny, is a brother," and "an Arab infidel, even if he was an Iraqi our enemy (sic)." The logic is that is "the nationality binding this ummah is Islam and only Islam."[98]

The Dangers of the Ideology

This ideology is particularly dangerous for several reasons. It has wide appeal because it portrays Muslims as victims; and it provides them a common enemy in the form of all non-Muslims. Its proposed solutions come from the Koran and hadith, sources with which all Muslims are familiar, even if they are uneducated. This ideology stresses the commitment of the individual Muslim as well as the collective Muslim community. Lastly, this ideology allows those who practice it, the justification under Islamic foundations to declare anyone, either Muslim or non-Muslim, as their enemy.

Ideology as the unifying agent. In *Ideology and Discontent*, David Apter states, "Ideology links particular actions and mundane practices with a wider set of meanings and, by doing so, lends a more honorable and dignified complexion to social conduct. From another vantage point, ideology may be viewed as a cloak for shabby motives and appearances."[99] This insight shows how an ideology can serve both as a doctrine and as vehicle for rationalizing or justifying actions under the guise of some principle of higher calling.

The current situation in Iraq supports Aptner's theory. To Zarqawi, bin Laden, Zawahiri, and their ilk, the ideology stands alone and does not have to fill a particular vacancy or serve as an alternative way to achieve their desired goal. To the radicals this is their *raison d'être*. Moreover, while they truly believe in their ideology, they accept short-term support from those who may not necessarily be fully committed to their ideology or tactics.

The authors of *In Their Own Words* show how this radical ideology crosses the boundaries and serves as "a cloak in shabby motives and appearances" to those Muslims who at some level disagree with either the tactics or ideology. This report says:

> "The influence of (radical Islamism) reached beyond
> groups that formally identify themselves as such. (Radical
> Islamism) benefits from the strength of the weak ties: the
> ability to bind together people who may share little else.
> On the one hand, requirements for being a good Muslim
> (and even the best of Muslims) are simple and easily met,
> since fighting a jihad satisfies the obligations of a pious
> life. On the other hand, because the focus is on duplicating
> the personal behaviors and moral code of early Muslims …,
> (radical Islamism) is an essentially apolitical doctrine and
> therefore avoids potential divisive issues.[100]

Bernard Lewis, a noted writer of theology and Islam, states, "Religious fundamentalism enjoys several advantages against competing ideologies. It is readily intelligible to both educated and uneducated Muslims. It offers a set of themes, slogans, and symbols that are profoundly familiar and therefore effective in mobilizing support and in formulating both a critique of what is wrong and a program for putting it right."[101]

Legitimacy. Ideology is the primary basis for legitimacy within any insurgency.

Regarding the Iraqi insurgency, Shmeul Bar states, "The moral justification and levers of

power for these movements, however, were for the most part not couched in political

term, but based on Islamic religious sources of authority and religious principles. By

using these levers and appealing to deeply ingrained beliefs, the radical leaders succeed

in motivating the Islamist terrorist, creating for him a social environment that provides

approbation and a religious environment that provides moral and legal sanctions for his

actions."[102] This observation shows that by couching their ideals, complaints, and goals

in Islamic terms, insurgent leaders are able to establish the legitimacy required to recruit,

operate, and sustain the insurgency.

   Besides internal legitimacy, an organization must also have recognized legitimacy

and recognition beyond its own confines. Noted author and analyst Loretta Napoleoni

says, "Lacking religious authority, (Zarqawi) was unable to rally the Iraqi Sunni

population. His leadership needed legitimacy and that could be provided only by Al-

Qaeda. From August 2003, Zarqawi repeatedly sought bin Laden's approval and

recognition."[103]

   Bin Laden provided Zarqawi this much-needed legitimacy in a taped message in

October 2004. Yasir al-Sirri, a London based activist, reinforces the significance of this

recognition in an 18 October 2004 Al Jeerza article titled "Zarqawi: Allegiance to Al-

Qaeda." Sirri claims that this taped message "is aimed at boosting morale and recruiting

more people by saying that Tawid and Jihad have become the soldiers of bin Laden in

Iraq."[104] Clearly, Zarqawi understands that both internal and external legitimacy are

critical requirements for the success of his cause.

Another important and dangerous aspect of this ideology is that it legitimizes, advocates, and condones the use of suicide bombing along with attacks against civilian targets. While these radical Islamists cannot claim that they originated such practices, they can certainly make the claim that they are the current masters of the art. Again referring to Cordesman, we find that the ingenuity, sophistication, and lethality of these devices coupled with the delivery and detonation techniques far surpasses the level of violence that proceeded Iraq.[105]

Appeal of the Ideology. "There are of course, many reasons why religion is so adept at mobilizing its followers and inspiring them to fight, to the death if necessary. Religion persuades individuals that it is worth both killing and dying for. These are the very ideologies that play a part in terrorist recruitment today as they have for thousands of years, throughout the history of the religious traditions."[106] These comments by Dr. J.P. Larson, a researcher who works for the British government, demonstrate how the insurgency leadership can motivate and recruit a seemingly endless supply of volunteers to their cause.

Individually, this ideology promises instant glorification and self-worth to the followers who participate in jihad. As a result, participation in support of a jihad appeals directly to the individual sense of purpose and esteem. "The use of religious concepts like jihad and martyrdom to justify and legitimate suicide bombing provides a powerful incentive: the prospect of being glorified hero in this life and enjoying paradise in the next."[107] Zarqawi is both prolific and proactive in his public announcements to support the insurgents and denounce his enemies. In a recent taped message released to Al

Jeerza, Zarqawi likes the current struggle as the "new Crusades raging into the Land of the Two Rivers, and it (United States) aspires to empower Jews and seeks to prolong its monopoly by controlling the richest country in the world." Later, Zarqawi claims, "By his very nature the ordinary and upright Muslim loves jihad and wants to participate in efforts to worship god against all sorts of infidelism. In order to let some steam out of the pots, some clever and devious methods are used."[108]

According to Leonard Weinberg in "Political and Revolutionary Ideologies," "This type of ideology furnishers it members with an exaggerated sense of importance and as such believe that they have the means to achieve great things. As a result, these groups are able to achieve a kind of elitist spirit de corps." Additionally, Weinberg says, "The ideologies offer a pathway to power. The terrorism will raise the level of awareness and trigger a violent uprising, from proletarian insurrection to racial holy war, by a vast pool of supporters previously too victimized and too lacking the required audacity ... to take the initiative."[109]

Most westerns and even some Muslims familiar with Zarqawi's and bin Laden's references to the Koran and the hadith, argue that these references are inaccurate or taken out of context. But as Jessica Stern points out in her insightful book, *Terror in the name of God*, the effectiveness of the message is always more important than its contextual accuracy. Sterns correctly identifies that, "The problem is that the (radical) Islamists are able to persuade their followers that they are preaching Islam, even if they are reading the texts selectively. All religious terrorists engage in hermeneutics (interpreting texts) ...but (radical) Islamists seem to be able to spread their message to a larger group of followers..."[110]

Declaring others illegitimate. As is common with most religiously based ideologies, the radical Islamists in Iraq consider themselves superior to others. Moreover, when others fail to support or worse, openly challenge them, the natural defense mechanism of the radicals is to declare the challenger an enemy. Typically, religiously based groups such as Al Qaeda tend to use religiously charged terms in an effort to demonize the enemy.[111] This type of de-humanization is evident on a taped Al Qaeda declaration from 6 July 2005. According to the speaker on the tape, purported to be Zarqawi, "We announce that the Iraqi army is an army of apostates and mercenaries that has allied itself with the Crusaders and came to destroy Islam and fight Muslims. We will fight it.... God has ordered us to fight the non-believers....We think that the nation is committing a sin by failing to support the mujahidin."[112]

Another example of this type of exclusivist attitude is evident on a 14 September 2005 recording, also purported to be al-Zarqawi, that states, "Any religious group that wants to be safe from the blows of the mujahid must (disavow) the government of al-Jaafari and it crimes. Otherwise it will suffer the same fate as that of the crusaders." Later the recording states, "Any tribe ... whose allegiance to the crusaders and their agent is proven will be targeted by the mujahid in the same way the crusaders are."[113]

It is evident that the use of terms such as crusaders, apostates, and non-believers is a deliberate effort to demonize the U.S. and Iraqi forces and simultaneously provide motivation and legitimacy to the insurgents.

Promoting the Ideology

Imams. The other key component for acceptance and legitimacy is through the support and endorsement of imams and religious scholars. According to Michael Radu in "Radical Imams and Terrorists," "The legitimizers and bearers of (radical) Islamism are religious figures – the radical imams…Without them, the entire ideological, political, and psychological edifice of Islamism would crumble."[114] Zarqawi and others routinely quote endorsements and quotations from imams who support their cause. Additionally, these imams and others will often make public declarations of support in the larger prayer services, typically held at noon on Fridays.[115]

In addition to providing theological legitimacy, the imams are an essential tool for the recruitment and motivation of the public. "The mosque is indeed coming back as a centre for political agitation and mobilization."[116] As Brachman and McCants report in *Stealing Al Qaeda's Playbook*, "Religious leaders play a critical role in attracting youth to the movement, providing religious justification for violence, and determining its overall strategic direction."[117]

A particularly illuminating example of the relationship between the imams and the insurgents was a recent broadcast by Al Qaeda of Iraq. This call publicly challenged and questioned the imams regarding their lack of support for the insurgency's on-going efforts. In the Foreign Broadcasts Information Service (FBIS) transcript titled "A Military Leader within Zarqawi's Group Appeals to Muslim Scholars" asks, "Have we accused you of non-belief, oh, virtuous ones? Or have fought on your behalf to protect your honor, your women, and your children? Oh Scholars, I ask you in the name of God

... Isn't our jihad in Iraq a legitimate jihad? And if the answer is yes, why did you leave us in Al-Qaim, Rawah, and Hasibah the way you left us in Fallujah, Samarra, and Tall Afar? "[118]

Madrasas. In addition to the imams, the madrasas, the historic educational institution in the Arab World, also provide legitimacy and support is for both the insurgency and the violent ideology that underpins it. These institutions, house, feed, and educate their students primarily from alms donated by the local population. Religious scholars and imams from the local mosque tend to serve as the instructors of most madrasas. Typical madrasa instruction includes Koranic memorization and recitation as well as practices of the hadith as interpreted by the madrasa's imam. "Defenders of the madrasas system view its traditional pedagogical approach as a way to preserve an authentic Islamic heritage."[119]

Jessica Stern, in "Preparing for a War on Terrorism" and Alan Richards in "War with Utopian Fanatics" argue madrasas provide very little education and instead teach primarily violence and anti-western feelings. However, most of their evidence that supports these claims is primarily anecdotal and refers mainly to madrasas in other countries such as Pakistan, Sudan, Syria, and others. Some claim this lack of factual evidence is primarily due to the restriction of most media sources from entering, attending, or documenting the madrasa's lectures and lessons.[120]

Despite the lack of factual evidence proving that the madrasas in Iraq serve as "seed corn" for the Iraq insurgency, one should recognize that as a minimum, the consolidated audience of a madrasa and the influence of the imam are a potent and potential combination that the insurgency will exploit if able.

An Updated Strategy

The challenge now is the development of a winnable strategy, assuming, of course, that the war is winnable. As Stephen Biddle, a Professor at the US Army War College, writes, "In fact this war can be won … But it will require war aims focused on our enemies' ideology, not their tactics. And this in turn will demand an especially close interconnection between a war of military violence and an inseparable war of ideas."[121]

At this point is it necessary to define clearly, what victory is. Due to the very nature of an ideological war, the author does not believe that any country including the United States can defeat an ideology, in the classical sense of the word. Ideology, as an entity, is indestructible and undefeatable in a physical sense. Rather, the best the United States can hope for is to diminish the appeal of this radical ideology so that is controllable at a local level. In this case, local level refers to law enforcement activities. It will take decades, if not longer, to effectively change the ideas present within a community, culture, or faith. The definition of victory in Iraq then, is not the defeat of the ideology, but the reduction and control of the ideology so that it no longer has its support or influence within Iraq.

According to J. Michael Barrett, a former Senior Analysts for the Global War on Terrorism to the Joint Chiefs of Staff, "The United States must pursue a two-pronged approach that diminishes the appeal of the ideology while simultaneously defeating the core element of the insurgency."[122] Barrett's comments reinforce the idea that the United States cannot have a strategy that is one dimensional, i.e. defeating the core elements of the insurgency. Barrett gives the ideological dimension equal if not higher priority than the physical dimension.

Likewise, Jason Burke, author of *Al Qaeda – Casting a Shadow of Terror,* understands the complexities of the situation, and stresses that military goals and actions are subordinate to the ideological dimension of the conflict. Burke writes:

> "…of course war should have a military component. It is easy to underestimate the sheer efficacy of military power in achieving specific immediate goals. Hardened militants cannot be rehabilitated and need to be made to cease their activities. But to win the battle our strategies must be made broader and more sophisticated. Military power must be only one tool among many, and a tool that is only rarely, and reluctantly used. Moderate Muslim leaders must be engaged, the spread of hard-line stands of Islam rolled back and an enormous effort to counter the growing sympathy for Al Qaeda's worldview must be made."[123]

Burke concludes that regardless of the chosen strategy, the United States will not be successful against the true believers of the ideology. Rather the United States and Iraq can only defeat people such as Abu Mus'ab Al-Zarqawi and his hard-core radicals through physical means, such as death or imprisonment.[124] Therefore, the development of strategy along ideological lines designed "to win the hearts and minds" of the Iraqis should focus on the defeat of those supporting the insurgency and on preserving the neutrality of remaining Iraqi population.

Therefore, a strategy aimed to reduce or control the radical ideology in Iraq must accomplish two primary goals: 1) it must decrease the appeal and legitimacy of the ideology; and 2) it must remove and replace the sources that promote this ideology. In order for the United States to win the ideological war in Iraq, and achieve victory as defined here, it needs to accomplish four major tasks.

First, the United States and Iraq remove the insurgency leadership and the hard-core radicals. These insurgents have committed themselves to fight and will not surrender. This means the United States and Iraqi forces will mostly likely have to kill or capture the majority of these fighters.

Second, the United States and Iraq must engage both the Iraqi and larger Muslim communities to denounce the ideology and reduce its appeal. These denouncements need to identify the differences between common Islamic teaching and the radical version of Islam the insurgency uses for its justification and legitimacy.

Third, the Iraqi government with the support of the religious scholars and the Iraqi population must take the necessary steps to silence those within the Iraqi population who advocate this ideology.

Finally, the United States and its allies need to continue in the establishment of a safe and viable environment within Iraq. This means that Iraq will need to establish and enforce the rule of law, even if it is a version of Islamic law. Additionally, the United States and its allies will need to continue to re-establish a viable economic system within Iraq. Physical security and a dependable economy will all but eliminate the large sections of the disenfranchised Iraqi community, who are likely to succumb to the appeal and attractiveness of this ideology.

Removing the Leadership and Hardcore Insurgents

The current efforts to capture or kill these leaders have been modestly effective to this point. However, the amount of resources required and the ability to dedicate them solely to this mission has not been supportable given the limited available resources and the security environment. As more Iraqi security forces become adequately trained and proficient, these forces should replace U.S. forces in their current role. Once the transition has occurred, U.S. forces along with specially trained Iraqi forces will focus exclusively on targeting, capturing, or killing high value target insurgents such as Abu Mu'sab al-Zarqawi.

In addition to increasing the effort to target such high profile personnel, the United States also needs to ensure that it both increases and leverages the capabilities of other agencies and elements with Iraq. The United States does not and most likely will not possess the skill and knowledge to evaluate and determine who they have captured and how important that person is within the insurgency. These efforts must focus not only on capturing such insurgents, but also on the identification, and retention of such captives. These improvements will reduce the likelihood of the inadvertent release of high value targets. This was the case in 2005 when the fledging Iraqi police force detained and then released Zarqawi from custody. Mistakes such as this only further discredit the United States and further bolster the insurgency.

Engaging the Muslims

The United States cannot defeat this insurgency without leveraging or at least neutralizing the power of the Islamic clergy. To this end, the United States and the Iraqi government efforts should primarily focus on religious leadership to discredit and de-legitimize the actions and proclamations of the insurgents. Secondary efforts should engage both the Iraqi population and the larger Muslim community to accomplish similar results. Finally, the United States must develop a coherent supporting strategy for its Information Operations (IO). This supporting strategy must be something more robust and creative than the past Public Diplomacy programs, whose performance was marginal at best.

Religious Leaders. It is a severe miscalculation to underestimate the power of the religious leadership. According to *Stealing Al Qaeda's Playbook*, one of the primary lessons learned from several failed Islamic insurgencies is the necessity for the insurgency "is to keep Muslims clerics actively involved."[125] As previously introduced evidence shows, the insurgency needs continuous reinforcement from the religious leaders for both its legitimacy and its actions.

These religious endorsements are both a critical requirement and vulnerability to the Iraqi insurgency. Therefore, the United States must exploit this vulnerability to the greatest degree possible. This means that coalition forces must directly interface with religious leaders within Iraq and the Muslim World. This interaction does not mean U.S. military commanders demanding to talk to imams or ayatollahs; rather it means that a variety of representatives, depending on the circumstances should engage these religious leaders to undermine the insurgency.

The Silent Iraqi Community. Cheryl Benard, a senior political scientist and director for Middle Eastern affairs at RAND Corporation, in *Democracy and Islam: The struggle in Islamic World* aggregated the Islamic world across a spectrum from fundamentalism to secularism. The spectrum Benard used established the divisions within Islamic ideologies and reflected which divisions shared similar democratic values. (See figure 4).

According to this analysis, the majority of the Islamic community is receptive to supporting the United States democratic message and will similarly be receptive to denouncing the actions and ideology of the insurgents that is counter to these shared ideals. However, the reality of the Iraqi situation is more complex and the Islamic community seems more reluctant than Benard's analysis suggests. As some have observed, it seems that the only times most moderate Muslim leadership, religious or political, choose to condemn certain actions or activities is when there is a large number of deaths or if a particular event touches upon certain sectarian issues.[126]

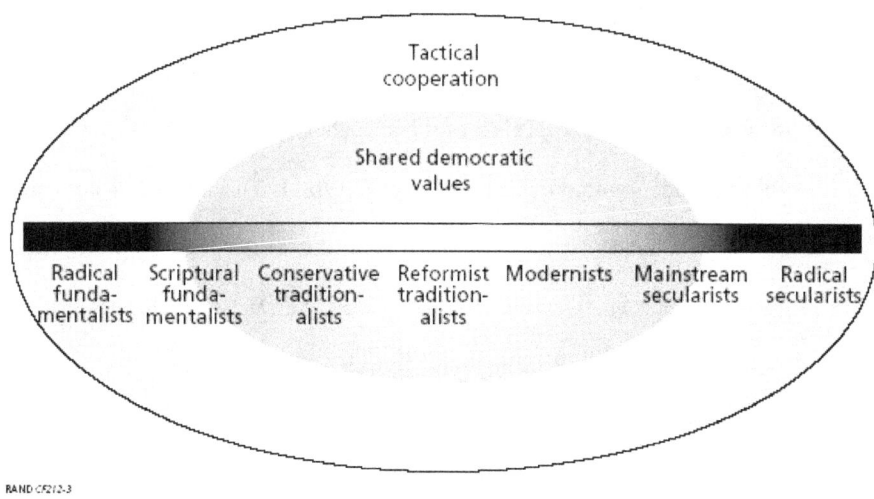

RAND CF212-3

Figure 4 -Ideological Spectrum for Contemporary Islamic Views

The lack of security within Iraq definitely precludes a majority of these leaders from speaking out. The threat to these leaders is very real. While various sources disagree on the validity, number of deaths, or the number of threats, it is a verifiable fact that religious leaders are subject to targeting and assassination. Even such prominent religious figures as the Grand Ayatollah Ali-al-Sistani, the highest-ranking Shia religious leader in Iraq, have been subject to both verbal and physical threats.[127] If the lack of security is a reason why such religious leaders do not speak out, then it reinforces the idea that the United States needs to have a comprehensive strategy that addresses both the physical and the ideological aspects of the insurgency.

Another potential reason why Iraq's religious leaders have not spoken out against either the insurgents or their tactics, is that these religious leaders may, to some extent, agree with the insurgents. While not necessarily, agreeing with the tactics or with the ideology, these leaders at least agree in principle with the concept of the defensive jihad against the occupation and presence of United States forces.

A clear example of this recently appeared in Al-Jeerza. In an article by Soumayya Ghannoushi titled "Al-Qaeda: The Wrong Answers," the author disparages Al Qaeda, their use of violence, their misinterpretation of Islam, and the killing of civilians. However, she very clearly states that her disagreement is not with the cause; rather it is with the means. Specifically, she is referring to the targeting of civilians and the killing of innocents in New York, London, and Madrid. Ghannoushi claims, "These are illegitimate responses to legitimate causes. Just as an occupation is morally and politically deplorable, so to is the blind aggression masquerading as jihad."[128]

Although there are no significant examples of religious leaders de-legitimizing or denouncing the tactics or the ideology of the insurgents, there are several instances where these same leaders have spoke out and de-escalated certain situations. These incidents include the sectarian violence from 25 to 28 February 2006 that resulted in the death of over 3000 Iraqi's.

The Vocal outside Community. Besides the religious leadership within Iraq, the United States must also capitalize on opportunities available from the larger Muslim world. One such example was following the bombing of a Mosque in Istanbul, Turkey. Selahattin Ozguduz, the leader of the Shiite Jafaris in Turkey, openly denounced the violence and ideology associated with the Iraq insurgency. Ozguduz, who studied at a Shiite madrasa in Iraq, stated. "They were the ones who perpetrated September 11 and the bombing incidents in Istanbul. It is time for the Islamic world to settle accounts with this gang." Ozguduz continued to de-legitimize the ideology as well as Zarqawi's and bin Laden's claims to religious authority when he warned, "We have to be alert against this mentality."[129]

Another opportunity in which the United States failed to capitalize on Islamic religious leadership speaking out against radical Islamic ideology was following the bombing of the Mosque in Sharm, Lebanon. In response to the bombing, Lebanon's most senior Shiite cleric, Grand Ayatolllah Mohammed Hussein Fadlallah – who had past connections with Hezbollah, but broke with the group – said that all Muslims must condemn such attacks, which he blamed on "backward minds that do not understand Islamic texts."[130] While these examples may cite incidents geographically separate from Iraq, the United States should not underestimate the power of both the message and the authority that sends it.

That these leaders are speaking out is the first crucial step towards discrediting the ideology, what the United States needs to do is further disseminate and broadcast such pronouncements when they occur. Instead of having radio stations and newspapers broadcasts the messages and interviews of Americans and other coalition members, our Strategic Information Operations should focus on the broadcasting of Muslims speaking out against the ideology and tactics of the insurgency, whenever possible.

Engaging other Leaders. While the recommendations thus far have focused primarily on religious leadership, this should not suggest that the United States Strategy be one-dimensional. Another potential opportunity for the U.S. to leverage in Iraq is the leadership of tribes and other affiliations that bisect the religious sector.

The United States successfully used this technique as part of its strategy in Afghanistan to defeat the Taliban and Al Qaeda. However, the United States has not clearly articulated or visibly pursued this as a potential advantage in Iraq. Based on previous experiences and similar circumstances, it seems the United States can use these alliances to help defeat the insurgency by minimizing the appeal of the ideology.

Successful implementation of the U.S. "rewards" program has significant potential for success. However, it will require the United States Government to adequately resource the federal agency it nominates as the lead for these programs. It the past, U.S. agencies have met with mixed results on such programs. The successful capture of Saddam Hussein and the targeting of his two sons are the highest profile successes to date within Iraq. To the contrary, anecdotal information suggests that beyond these limited successes, these programs typically fail due to lack of resources, primarily human resources, to process and handle the overwhelming response by the Iraqi public.[131]

Remembering that this insurgency is primarily about power and not religion provides the United States with another possible avenue to diminish the appeal of the ideology. *Stealing Al Qaeda's Playbook* states, "It is bad for the (insurgent) movement when the United States operates clandestinely or through proxies, whether they be local regimes, tribes, or ethnic minorities – (insurgents) have nothing to rally the public against and will be seen as fighting their own people."[132] Given this insight, it is apparent that the United States can empower elements with Iraq, whether they are tribal, ethnic, or religious, so long as they are supportive of the Iraqi government and oppose the insurgency.

Considering the complexity of the situation in Iraq, the United States should carefully endorse and support any Muslim religious leaders, inside or outside of Iraq, as well as tribal or ethnic leaders whose movements or causes effectively diminish the ideological strength of the insurgency. As the authors of *Stealing Al Qaeda's Playbook* state, "Naturally, many of the most effective competitors will not be friendly to the United States and the West; but if the bottom line is a rejection of violence against the United States and its allies, they should be supported."[133]

Silencing the advocates

In a recent *Arab Studies Quarterly* article, Ibrahm Elnur states the importance of countering those who promote the ideology and reducing their influence on the population and the insurgents. According to Elnur, "Undermining the basis for such claims to "justice" and "legitimacy" is the only way to eliminate their implicit or explicit characterization of their acts as being a public good."[134]   Michael Radu goes one step further and states, "It thus follows that any long-term solution to the threat of Islamist terrorism has to start with Islam's radical clerics…In contrast, the terrorist operatives themselves most obviously those willing to commit suicide, are expendable, since their motivators and recruiters can always produce more – and they always do."[135]

With Radu's insight as a backdrop, the Iraqi security forces with the support of United States military forces need to stop the imams and other religious spokespersons from directly inciting participation or advocating support for the insurgency. Accomplishment will require the co-option, coercion, or imprisonment of the imams in question. Additionally, steps of this nature will require establishing acceptable standards and preferably laws that prohibit both the solicitation and participation of insurrection, sedition, or other acts against the state. While this is not an easy task to accomplish, other Middle Eastern countries such as Jordan, Egypt, Algeria, and Morocco have established laws and routinely imprison imams who advocate or incite subversion of the national government.[136]

Michael Radu describes several recent examples where Arab nations have demonstrated the resolve to make these actions a reality. Radu writes:

> "When imams, legitimate or not, go beyond the limits
> tolerated by Muslim states, those governments take
> decisive action. "Thus, when Muslim "scholar" Abdul
> Rehman of Pakistan organized a widely attended service
> for Shehzad Tanweer, one of the London suicide terrorists,
> he was arrested; when Ali Belhandj, the former number two
> of the banned Islamic Salvation Front (FIS) of Algeria,
> supported the murder of Algerian diplomats in Iraq, he was
> arrested; when Yemeni cleric Ali Yahya supported the

rebellion led by the Zaidi cleric Sheikh Badr a-Din al-Huthi, he was sentenced to death."[137]

Reducing the Potential Insurgents

Finally, the United States and Iraq need to reduce the number of potential insurgents. While economic prosperity, political representation, and security will neutralize most of Iraq's disgruntled population, it will not satisfy all of them. There will still be a core of young men that are susceptible to radical teachings that promote violence and the spread of anarchy. To target this group, the United States and Iraq must offer alternative education options vis-à-vis existing madrasas. The insurgency and radical imams have historically used these madrasas to encourage and actively recruit Muslim's to join the jihad.

The first step in this process is the establishment of formalized standards and practices for imams and scholars to follow. Following the establishment and implementation of these standards, imams would be subject to review and disciplinary action. Once suspected of violating the standards, the imam is subject to dismissal or legal action, depending on the severity.

Another alternative is the establishment of new schools. These new construction facilities can be of modern design or of the traditional madrasa style, whichever the local community prefers. The government or senior religious officials within the nation would identify and select the imams and religious scholars to establish and teach at these new schools. Additional benefits of establishing new madrasas include greater educational opportunities for more Iraqis and the associated economic benefits that accompany

increased employment rates and new construction.

Conclusion

US forces can win every clash and encounter and still decisively lose the war after the war.[138]

-Dr. Anthony Cordesman

Despite the mounting political pressure and eroding public support, the United States can still win the war in Iraq. However, to do so, the United States must expand its current strategy to include the ideological dimension of the war. The defeat of this radical Islamic ideology is essential for victory in Iraq. As long as the ideology survives, people like Mus'ab al-Zarqawi and Osama bin Laden will continue to hijack Islam and manipulate its teachings for their own political gain or purpose.

This new revised United States strategy must include not only the ideological dimension of the war, but it must also provide positive steps and actions to accelerate the establishment of a stable and secure environment. With the establishment of a secure environment, at least at the local level, the new United States strategy will simultaneously achieve four primary tasks: targeting the insurgency's key leaders, engaging the Muslim community, silencing the advocates for violence, and reducing the number of potential insurgents.

Adoption of this strategy and its integration within the larger United States strategy will provide the United States a clear and concise way to achieve its desired goals in Iraq. Unless the United States understands, appreciates, and incorporates the ideological element into its analyses and strategies, it will be doomed to similar circumstances and situations like those we are currently experiencing in Iraq.

NOTES

[1] Mark Sappenfeld. "Military Strategy in Iraq: What Is It?" *Christian Science Monitor,* (17 October 2005): 17.

[2] See Defeating the Jihadists – A Blueprint for Action. (New York, The Century Foundation Press, 2004); Michael E. O'Hanlon. *Policy Review,* Iss. 128, (Dec 2004/ Jan 2005); and Dr. Anthony H. Cordesman written statement to the Committee on Foreign Relations United States Senate "An Effective Us Strategy for Iraq," (1 February 2005).

[3] For a comprehensive review of Iraq, its culture, and the forces that influence it today, sees William R. Polk, Understanding Iraq. (New York, Harper Collins Publishers, 2005).

[4] The mandate referred to here, is the League of Nations Mandate of 1920, this mandate granted the United Kingdom the authority to define and create the nation of Iraq following the defeat of the Ottoman Empire in World War I. (Accessed at http://www.countrywatch.com/cw_topic.aspx?type=text&vcountry=81&topic=POHIS on 1 Mar 2006.

[5] Michael Eisenstadt and Jeffrey White, "Assessing Iraq's Sunni Arab Insurgency," *The Washington Institute for Near East Policy Focus #50,* (December 2005): 11-13.

[6] Iraq is approximately 49% Shia and approximately 28% Arab Sunni. The Kurds, who are also Sunni Muslims, make up another 19%, although the Kurds do not associate or consider themselves part of the larger Iraqi Sunni population. Christianity and Judaism make up less than 3%. These estimates are based on the United Nations Development program, *Iraq Living Conditions Survey 2004.* (Available on line at http://www.iq.undp.org/ILCS/overview.htm). 15-19.

[7] Daniel Brumberg, "Islam is Not the Solution (or the Problem)," *The Washington Quarterly,* (Winter 2005-06): 98.

[8] Jonathan Finer and Naseer Nouri, "Loyalties Lie with Clerics, Not with Politicians, In Najaf." *Washington Post,* 17 October 2005, 11.

[9] John L. Esposito, "Contemporary Islam – Reformation or Revolution?" in The Oxford History of Islam. Ed. by John L. Esposito, (Oxford, Oxford Press, 2002): 645.

[10] Ibid, 644-645.

[11] Steven Metz, "Insurgency and Counterinsurgency in Iraq," *The Washington Quarterly,* (Winter 2003-04): 28.

[12] Richard A. Clarke et al., Defeating the Jihadists – A Blueprint for Action, (New York, The Century Foundation Press, 2004): 1.

[13] Clarke, et al: 87.

[14] Michael Eisenstadt and Jeffrey White: 4.

[15] The Kurds, a large ethnic population that is increasingly gaining political power in Iraq have successfully avoided becoming involved in the Iraq insurgency.

[16] Colonel W. Patrick Lang, USA, "Occupied Iraq – One Country Many Wars," *Middle East Policy* Vol XII, No. 3, (Fall 2005): 20.

[17] Jason Burke, Al Qaeda - Casting a Shadow of Terror, (New York, I.B Tauris, 2003): 5.

[18] Brian Michael Jenkins, "Can the Beast be Tamed?" *Boston Globe,* 18 May 2005, 1.

[19] The term insurgent will be used as defined; however, there may be instances where individuals or certain groups need to be individually identified. In these cases, the individual or group will be identified specifically by name and annotated as part of the larger Iraqi insurgency.

[20] Merriam Webster's Collegiate Dictionary, 11th ed. (Springfield, MS, Merriam –Webster, Inc., 2003): 649. The DOD definition from Jt. Pub 1-02 Definition of Terms is too narrow and does not sufficiently address the current enemy in Iraq.

[21] See Anthony Cordesman, Iraq's Evolving Insurgency: The Nature of Attacks and Patterns and Cycles in the Conflict. (Washington D.C., Center for Strategic and International Studies, Working Draft, revised: February 3, 2006).

[22] Henry Shuster, "Iraq Insurgency 101," CNN, 12 October 2005. Accessed on 23 February 2006 at http://www.cnn.com/2005/WORLD/meast/10/12/schuster.column/index.html.

[23] International Crisis Group, "In their Own Words: Reading the Iraqi Insurgency", *Middle East Report No. 50,* (15 February 2006): iii. Accessed at http://www.crisisgroup.org/home/index.cfm?id=3953&l=1 on 1 Mar 2006.

[24] Michael Eisenstadt and Jeffrey White, 3.

[25] Greg Miller and Tyler Marshall, "More Iraqis lured to Al Qaeda Group," *Los Angeles Times,* 16 September 2005. 1.

[26] International Crisis Group, 11.

[27] Cordesman, Iraq's Evolving Insurgency, iii.

[28] Ibid.

[29] Ahmed Hashim, "Iraq Insurgency is no Monolith," *National Catholic Reporter*, 26 September 2003. 23.

[30] Ibid.

[31] Bruce Hoffman, "Insurgency and Counterinsurgency in Iraq," *A RAND Occasional Paper*, (June 2004):6.

[32] Brumberg, 99.

[33] President George W. Bush, *National Strategy for Combating Terrorism*, (Washington D.C., US GPO, Februaury 2003): 11. Emphasis included in original text.

[34] Ibid, 13.

[35] John Parachini, Peter Wilson, and David Aaron, "Defeating the Global Jihadist Movement: Results of a RAND Exercise," *Three Years After –Next Steps in the War on Terror,* David Aaron Ed. (2005): 12.

[36] Ibid, 13.

[37] Bush, *National Strategy for Combating Terrorism*, 23-24.

[38] President George W. Bush, *National Strategy for Victory in Iraq*, (Washington D.C., National Security Council, November 2005): 6-7. Italics and bold are original emphasis.

[39] Ibid, 8.

[40] See Paul Wolfowitz, *A Strategic Approach to the Challenge of Terrorism.* (Speech presented to RAND Corporation, Grand Hyatt Washington, Washington D.C. 8 September 2004.) Secretary of Defense Rumsfeld "Secretary Rumsfeld Stakeout with U.S. Ambassador Zalmay Khalilzad and Gen. George Casey in Baghdad, Iraq" speech given on 27 July 2005. Secretary of State Rice, "75th Anniversery for the Woodrow Wilson School of Public and International Affairs," presented at Princeton University on 30 September 2005.

[41] Kenneth Katzman, *Iraq U.S. Regime change Efforts and Post-Saddam Governance*, (Washington D.C., Congressional Research Service, updated 5 October 2005): CRS-31.

[42] Mark Sappenfeld. "Military Strategy in Iraq: What Is It?" *Christian Science Monitor,* 17 October 2005, 1.

[43] Rep Murtha, "War in Iraq," speech to Congress on 17 November 2005. Accessed at http://house.gov/apps/list/press/pa12-murtha/pr051117iraq.html on 16 January 2006.

[44] Ibid.

[45] David Broder, "Against the Tide in Iraq," *The Washington Post,* 20 November 2005, B07.

[46] Fareed Zakaria, "Finally a Smart Iraq Strategy," *Newsweek,* 24 October 2005, 33.

[47] *The 9/11 Commission's Report*, (Washington D.C., US GPO, 2003): 362. Emphasis and quotation is from original text. The author has replaced the original used term "Islamist terrorism" with "radical Islamist' to better reflect this ideology and further differentiate it from the beliefs and teachings of Islam.

[48] Of note are the activities and teachings of Sayd Qutb. Qutb was an Egyptian activist who espoused the use of violence in pursuit of religious goals. The Egyptian government executed him in 1959 following an attempted assassination of the Egypt President. Qutb authored several books including "Signs," which is often quoted by the radical Islamists.

[49] The 9/11 Commission's Report, 579, The term caliphate refers to the establishment of an Islamic empire ruled by Muslims and under Islamic law, or sharia. The last caliphate ended with the break up of the Ottoman Empire following World War I.

[50] Ibid.

[51] Shmuel Bar, "The Religious sources of Islamic Terrorism," *Policy Review*, (June & July 2004): 27.

[52] President George W. Bush, quoted from a town hall meeting in Ontario, California 5 January 2005. Accessed at http://www.whitehouse.gov/infocus/ramadan/islam.html. on 28 February 2006.

[53] Bar, "The Religious Sources of Islamic Terrorism," 28.

[54] Paul Marshall, "The Islamists' Other Weapon," *Commentary,* Vol. 199, Iss. 4 (April 2005): 60.

[55] Bar, 28.

[56] Ibid.

[57] David Little, "Phenomena of Faith – Religious Dimensions of Conflicts and Peace," *Harvard International Review*, (Winter 2005): 22.

[58] George W. Bush, Speech given to the National Endowment for Democracy, 6 October 2005, accessed at http://www.whitehouse.gov/news/releases/2005/10/20051006-3.html on 16 January 2006.

[59] The term "religious influenced" is a term used by Dr. David Little in "Phenomena of Faith – Religious Dimensions of Conflicts and Peace."

[60] Grant Highland, "The Global Insurgency within Islam," *Essays 2003 – Chairman of the Joint Chiefs of Staff Strategy Essay Competition*, (Washington D.C., National Defense University Press, 2003): 19.

[61] Title burrowed from the anonymous book titled *Thorough Our Enemies' Eyes*, (Washington D.C., Brassey's Inc., 2002).

[62] Ralph Peters, "Rolling Back Radical Islam," *Parameters*, (Fall 2002): 4.

[63] Christopher M. Blanchard, "Al Qaeda: Statements and Evolving Ideology," *CRS Report for Congress* (4 February 2005).

[64] Ibid, 6.

[65] Amman and Brussels, "In their Own Words: Reading the Iraqi Insurgency," *Middle East Report* No 50, (International Crisis Croup, 15 February 2006): 5. Accessed at http://www.crisisgroup.org/home/index.cfm?id=4028&l=1 on 4 March 2006.

[66] Ibid, 7 – 11.

[67] Michael Eisenstadt and Jeffrey White, 31.

[68] Mark Juergensmeyer, "Terror in the Name of God," *Current History*, (November 2001): 358.

[69] Ibid, 358.

[70] Thorough Our Enemies' Eyes, (Washington D.C., Brassey's Inc., 2002): 256.

[71] Shmuel Bar, 27.

[72] Huston Smith, *Islam A Concise Introduction*. (San Francisco, CA, HarperSanFransico, 2001): 2.

[73] Particularly, all three religions are based on the descendants of Shem, one of Noah's sons. "This is where the word Semite comes from; literally a Semite is a descendant of Shem. Like the Jews, Arabs considered themselves a Semitic people." See Islam: a Concise Introduction by Huston Smith or The Oxford History of Islam ed. By John L. Esposito..

[74] Esposito, What Everyone needs to know about Islam, 39. Iraq is approximately 49% Shia and approximately 28% Arab Sunni. The Kurds, who are also Sunni Muslims, make up another 19%, although the Kurds do not associate or consider themselves part of the larger Iraqi Sunni population. Christianity and Judaism make up less than 3%.

[75] Fred M. Donner, "Muhammad and the Caliphate" in The Oxford History of Islam ed. by John L. Esposito, (Oxford, Oxford Press, 2002): 11.

[76] Esposito, What Everyone needs to know about Islam. Also see Fred M. Donner, "Muhammad and the Caliphate" in The Oxford History of Islam ed. by John L. Esposito, 1-61. Shias believe that their religious leaders, or Imams, are religiously inspired, sinless, and the interpreters of God's will as contained in Islamic law. Shias consider the sayings, deeds, and writings of their Imams to be authoritarian religious texts.

[77] P.J. Vatikiotis, "The Nature of Islam" in *Islam and Power*, edited by Cudsi and Dessouki, (Baltimore, MD, The Johns Hopkins University Press, 1981): 189.

[78] Esposito, What Everyone needs to know about Islam, (New York, Oxford University Press, 2002): 151. Parenthesis are in the original text.

[79] Ibid, 151.

[80] Brumberg, 98.

[81] Esposito, What Everyone needs to know about Islam, 118.

[82] See Rudolph Peters, Jihad in Classical and Modern Islam, (Princeton, N.J., Markus Weiner Publishing, 2005) and John L. Esposito, What Everyone needs to Know about Islam, and The Oxford History of Islam ed by John L. Esposito.

[83] Esposito, What Everyone needs to know about Islam, 118.

[84] Rudolph Peters, 1.

[85] Esposito, What Everyone needs to know about Islam, 118.

[86] Rudolph Peters, 1-8.

[87] Michael C. Fowler, *Amateur Soldiers, Global Wars*, (Westport CN. Praeger Security International, 2006): 146.

[88] See CNN Staff, *Al Qaeda in Iraq Issues Virulent Manifesto.* August 26, 2005. Accessed at www.cnn com/2005/world/meast/08/26/alqaeda.book/index.html on 6 January 2006.

[89] Esposito, What Everyone needs to know about Islam, 118.

[90] Ibid, 121-122.

[91] Leonard Weinberg, "Political and Revolutionary Ideologies," in The Making of a Terrorist, ed. By James J.F. Forest, (Westport CN, Praeger Security International, 2006): 182.

[92] Ralph Peters, "The Counterrevolution in Military Affairs," *The Weekly Standard,* 6 February 2006, 21.

[93] International Crisis Group, 2.

[94] S.V.R. Nasr, "European Colonialism and the Emergence of Modern Muslim States", *The Oxford History of Islam*, ed. By John Esposito, Oxford, Oxford Press, 2002. 565.

[95] Marc Sageman, "The Global Salafi Jihad," statement to the National Commission on Terrorist Attacks upon the United States, 9 July 2003. Accessed at http://www.9-11commission.gov/hearing/hearing3/witness-sageman.htm . on 15 Jan 2006.

[96] Ibid.

[97] John L. Esposito, What Everyone needs to know about Islam, 16.

[98] FBIS, "Al Zarqaw's Legal Council Defines 'Islamic Ummah,'" Accessed at https://www.fbis.gov GMP20051020371009 Jihadist Websites on 7 March 2006.

[99] David Aptner, *Ideology and Discontent* (Glencoe, IL., Free Press, 1964): 16.

[100] Amman & Brussels, 11. Salafism from the original text has been replaced with radical Islamism.

[101] Bernard Lewis, Crisis in Islam: Holy War and Unholy Terror, (New York, Modern library, 2003).

[102] Bar, 28.

[103] Loretta Napoleoni, "He's at the heart of Iraq's Troubles," *Independent on Sunday* (London), 12 November 2005, 21.

[104] Al Jazeera, "Al-Zarqawi: Allegiance to Al-Qaeda, 18 October 2004. Accessed at http://english.aljazeera.net/NR/exeres/E993984-2B6A-4106-9D7D-1503B28D8952.htm on 4 March 2006. Tawid and Jihad are the shortened names associated with two disparate insurgency groups that were operating independently in Iraq prior to this endorsement from Al-Qaeda. Tawid has since changed its name to "Al-Qaeda of Iraq" or "Al-Qaeda of the Two Rivers". The latter a reference to the land between the Tigris and Euphrates rivers.

[105] Cordesman, iii.

[106] J.P. Larson, "The Role of Religious Ideology in Modern Terrorist Recruitment," in The Making of a Terrorist: Recruitment, ed. By James J.F. Forest.(Westport CN, Praeger Security International, 2006): 198.

[107] Esposito, What Everyone needs to know about Islam, 126.

[108] FBIS, "Al-Zarqawi on US casualties in Iraq, Elections, Israel", 09 January 2006, Accessed at https://www.fbis.gov GMP20060109519001 Jihadist Websites on 17 Mar 2006.

[109] Leonard Weinberg, 195

[110] Jessica Stern, *Terror in the Name of God – Why Religious Militants Kill.* (New York, Harper Collins, 2003): 46-47.

[111] See Leonard Weinberg, 181 – 196.

[112] Al Jazeera, "Al-Zarqawi tape defends Iraq Attacks, 06 July 2005. Accessed at http://english.aljazeera net/NR/exeres/55FAF3A-B267-427A-B9Ec-54881BDE0A2E.htm on 4 March 2006.

[113] Al Jazeera, "Al-Zarqawi declares war on Iraqi Shia, 14 September 2005. Accessed at http://english.aljazeera net/NR/exeres/407AAE91-AF72-45D7-83E9-486063CoE5EA.htm on 4 March 2006.

[114] Michael Radu, "Radical Imams and Terrorists," Foreign *Policy Research Institute Newsletter,* Vol. 6 No. 6 (Aug 2005): 1-5. Accessed at http:/www.fpri.org/ww/0606.200508.radu.imamterrosits.htm on 15 September 2005.

[115] The Iraq Insurgency, History Channel film, 2005. Details eyewitness accounts of the relationship between imams and insurgents in Iraq.

[116] Alexander S. Cudsi and Ali E. Hillal Dessouki, *Islam and Power*, edited by Cudsi and Dessouki, (Baltimore MD, The Johns Hopkins University Press, 1981): 11.

[117] Jarret M. Brachman and William F. McCants, Stealing Al Qaeda's Playbook, (West Point NY, Counter Terrorism Center, 2005): 20.

[118] FBIS, "Military Leader in Al-Zarqawi's group Appeals to Muslim Scholars, 17 January 2006. Accessed at https://www.fbis.gov GMP20060117371014 Jihadist Websites on 7 March 2006

[119] Christopher M. Blanchard, "Islamic Religious Schools, Madrasas: Background," CRS Report for Congress, (updated 10 January 2006): 3.

[120] Jessica Stern, "Preparing for a War on Terrorism," current history, vol. 100, iss. 649 (Nov 2001): 353-355. Alan Richards, "At War with Utopian Fanatics," Middle East Policy, vol. VIII, no. 4 (Dec 2001): 5-10.

[121] Dr. Stephen Biddle, "War Aims and War Termination", in Defeating Terrorism: Strategic Issue Analysis, ed. by Col John R. Martin, (Carlisle Barracks, PA, Strategic Studies Institute, 2002): 7.

[122] J. Michael Barrett, "The Sources of Terrorist Conduct," Strategic Insights, Volume III, Issue 12 (December 2004): Accessed at www.ccc.nps.navy.mil/si/2004/dec/barrettdec04.pdf on 15 October 2005.

[123] Burke, 249.

[124] Ibid.

[125] Brachman and McCants, 17.

[126] These events include the targeting and killing of Muslims at mosques or other religious venues. The killing of non-Muslims also seems to reach this threshold when the event is of particular level of cruelty (the beheadings of Nicolas Berg and Daniel Pearl) or when the event is of global scale, such as the attacks on New York, Washington D.C., London, and Madrid.

[127] Various reports document different attacks on Grand Ayatollah Al-Sistani and other senior Shia religious leaders, including several assassination attempts.

[128] Soumayya Ghannoushi, "Al-Qaida: the Wrong Answers" Al-Jeerza, 11 July 2005. Accessed on 4 March 2006 at http://english.aljazeera.net/NR/exeres/554FAF3A-B267-427A-B9EC-54881DE0A2E.htm

[129] Ahmet Hakan, "Muslims Must Oppose the Al-Zarqawi Gang," Istanbul Hurriyet, 27 February 2006. Accessed on 7 March 2006, at https://www.fbis.gov GMP20060227016003

[130] Lee Keath, "Egypt's Top Islamic cleric delivers sermon against terrorism in wake of Sharm attacks," International News, (Cairo), 29 July 2005.

[131] L. Paul Bremer III with Malcolm McConnell, My Year in Iraq, (New York, Simon & Schuster, 2006): 107, 118, 264, 347. Amb. Bremer refers only to the successes of the reward program with regards to Saddam Hussein and his sons. Bremer does not talk about the failure and challenges of the reward program faced by the US State Department.

[132] Brachman and McCants, 18. The original text used "jihadis" to describe the ideological insurgents.

[133] Ibid, 20.

[134] Ibrahim Elnur, "11 September and the Widening North-South Gap: Root Causes of Terrorism in the Global Order," Arab Studies Quarterly, Volume 25, Numbers 1&2, (Winter/ Spring 2003): 58.

[135] Michael Radu, 1-5.

[136] Ibid 1-5.

[137] Ibid, 3-4.

[138] Dr. Anthony H. Cordesman, US Policy in Iraq: A "Realist" Approach to its Challenges and Opportunities, (Washington D.C., Center for Strategic and International Studies, revised 6 August 2004): 19.

Selected Bibliography

Andreani, Gilles, "The War on Terror: Good Cause; Wrong Concept." *Survival,* issue 46 no. 4 (winter 2004/2005): 31-50.

Bar, Shmeul, "The Religious Sources of Islamic Terrorism," *Policy Review* 125 (Jun / Jul 2004): 27-38.

Barrett, J. Michael, "The Sources of Terrorist Conduct," *Strategic Insights* vol. III, iss. 12 (Dec 2004).

Blanchard, Christopher M., *Al Qaeda: Statements and Evolving Ideology.* Washington D.C.: Congressional Research Report for Congress, updated February 4, 2005. Accessed at www ndu.edu/library/ docs/crs/crs-RL32759-04Feb05.pdf.

Brumberg, Daniel, "Islam is Not the Solution (or the Problem)," *The Washington Quarterly*, Winter 2005-06.

Burke, Jason. *Al Qaeda: Casting a Shadow of Terror.* New York: I.B. Tauris, 2003: iv, 65.

Cordesman, Anthony H., *"The Iraq War: Strategy Tactics and Military lessons."* Washington D.C.: Center for Strategic and International Studies, 2003. 148-165.
_____. *US Policy in Iraq: A "Realist" Approach to its Challenges and Opportunities*, Washington D.C.: Center for Strategic and International Studies, revised 6 August 2004.

Clarke, Richard, et. al. *Defeating the Jihadists – A Blueprint for Action.* New York: The Century Foundation Press, 2004.

Clausewitz, Carl Von. *On War.* Trans. Michael Howard & Peter Paret. New York: Alfred A. Knopf, 1993.

CNN Staff, *Al Qaeda in Iraq Issues Virulent Manifesto.* August 26, 2005. Accessed at www.cnn.com/2005/world/meast/08/26/alqaeda.book/index.html.

Colorado Springs Gazette, 3rd ACR Chief: Rebels Worst of the Worst," *Colorado Springs Gazette,* 14 September 2005.

Cragin, Kim and Scott Gerwehr, *Dissuading Terror: Strategic Influence and the struggle against Terrorism.* Washington D.C., RAND, 2004.

Crawford, Neta, "The Road to Global Empire: The Logic of US Foreign Policy after 9/11," *Orbis,* vol. 48 no. 4 (autumn 2004): 685-703.

Cronin, Audrey J., "Behind the Curve: Globalization and International Terrorism," *International Security,* Volume 27, no. 3 (winter 2002/2003): 45-54.

Cronin Audrey J. and James M. Lundes, eds. *Attacking Terrorism: Elements of Grand Strategy*. Washington D.C.: Georgetown University Press, 2004.

Djerejian, Edward P. et. al. *Changing Minds/ Winning Peace*. Report to the Advisory group on Public Diplomacy for the Arab and Muslim World. 1 Oct 2003: 8.

Dobbins, James, "Securing the Peace will require finesse," *Orange County Register,* 27 Jul 2004.

Donnelly, Thomas. *Naming the Enemy*. Washington D.C.: American Enterprise Institute for Public Policy Research, Aug 2004.

Donner, Fred. "Sources of Islamic Conceptions of War," *Just War and Jihad*. Edited by John Kelsay and James Turner Johnson. Westport, Conn: Greenwood Publishing Group, 1991. 31-33.

Eisenstadt, Michael and Jeffrey White, "Assessing Iraq's Sunni Arab Insurgency," *The Washington Institute for Near East Policy Focus #50*, December 2005.

Elnur, Ibrahim, "11 September and the Widening North-South Gap: Root Causes of Terrorism in the Global Order," *Arab Studies Quarterly,* vol. 25 no. 1 & 2, (winter/spring 2003): 57-70.

Esposito, John I. *The Oxford History of Islam*. New York: Oxford University Press, 1999: 675-680.

_____. *What Everyone Needs to Know About Islam*: New York: Oxford University Press, 2002.

Galloway, Joseph L., "Some Officers Believe the War 'Will Last for Years'." *Miami Herald*, 6 September 2005.

Ghent, Ralph D. "Issues on the Center of Gravity in CounterInsurgency Operations." Masters thesis Naval War College, 19 May 1997.

Gomez, Jamie Jr. "Terrorist Motivations for the use of Extreme Violence," *Strategic Insights* vol. IV, iss. 5, (May 2005).

Hafez, Mohammed. *Why do Muslims Rebel?* Boulder, CO.: Lynne Reinner Publishers, 2003: 199-200.

Handel, Michael I. *Masters of War – Classical Strategic Thought.* 3rd ed. Portland: Frank Cass, 2003.

Harvey, Thomas H. *Between Iraq and a Hard Place: US Policy towards Iraq*. Submission to National Defense University, November 2004.

Highland, Grant R. "New Century/ Old Problems: The Global Insurgency within Islam and the Nature of the War on Terror," *Essays 2003 - Chairman of the Joint Chiefs of Staff Strategy Essay Competition*. Washington D.C.: National Defense University Press, 2003:17-30.

Hoffman, Bruce. "Al Qaeda and the War on Terrorism – an update," *Current History*, Volume 103, number 677 (December 2004): 423-427.

_____. *Insurgency and Counterinsurgency in Iraq*. Washington D.C.: RAND Corporation, June 2004.

_____. "Lessons from the Past for Iraq's Future." *San Diego Union-Tribune*, 23 July 2004.

International Crisis Group, "In their Own Words: Reading the Iraqi Insurgency", *Middle East Report No. 50*, 15 February 2006.

Jenkins, Brian Michael, "Can the Beast be Tamed." *Boston Globe,* 18 May 2005.

_____. "Four Years after 9/11, War on Terror Slogs on." *San Diego Union-Tribune*, 11 September 2005.

Howard, Michael. "'9/11' and after: A British View." *Naval War College Review* 55, no. 4 (autumn 2002). 17.

Katzman, Kenneth, *Iraq: U.S. Regime Change efforts and Post-Saddam Governance.* Washington D.C.: Congressional Research Service, updated on October 5, 2004.

Kissinger, Henry. "America's Assignment." *Newsweek* vol. 144, iss. 19 (8 November 2004): 32.

Knapp, Michael G., "The Concept and Practice of Jihad in Islam," *Parameters* 1 (spring 2003): 82-94.

Krepinevich, Andrew F., "*Combating Terrorism*," March 03, 2003 testimony to committee on House Government Reform Sub-committee on National Security Emerging Threats, and International Relations. (Washington D.C., Center for Strategic Studies and Budgetary Assessments, 2003).

Lacquer, Walter. "The Terrorism to Come," *Policy Review* 126 (August / September 2004): 49-65.

_____. *Voices of Terror*. New York: Reed Press, 2004: 410-419.

Lewis, Bernard. *The Crisis of Islam – Holy War and Unholy Terror*. New York: Modern Library, 2003: 16-17, 133-165.

Lueking, Richard W. *Applying Operational Art to CounterInsurgency Campaign Planning*. Thesis Naval War College, 14 Jun 1996.

Mahmood, Iftekhar. *Islam – Beyond Terrorists and Terrorism*. Lanham, MD: University Press of America, 2002: xiv.

Marshall, Paul, "The Islamists' Other Weapon." *Commentary* vol. 119, iss. 4 (Apr 2005): 60-63.

Martin, John R. "Defeating Terrorism." *Strategic Issue Analysis*. Carlisle Barracks: Strategic Studies Institute, 2002: 1-20.

Metz, Steven, "Insurgency in Iraq," *The Washington Quarterly*, vol. 27, no. 1 (winter 2003/2004): 32.

Miller, Greg and Tyler Marshall. "More Iraqis lured to Al Qaeda Group." *Los Angeles Times,* 16 September 16 2005. 1.

Myers, Richard B. *The National Military Strategy of the United States of America – A Strategy for Today; A Vision for Tomorrow*. Washington, D.C.: GPO, 2004.

National Review editors, "Winning in Iraq," *National Review.* (July 18, 2005): 12-13.

O'Hanlon, Michael. "Iraq without a Plan," *Policy Review* 128 (December 2004/ January 2005): 33-47.

Parachini, John, Peter Wilson, and David Aaron, "Defeating the Global Jihadist Movement: Results of a RAND Exercise," *Three Years After –Next Steps in the War on Terror,* David Aaron Ed. Washington D.C.:, Rand, 2005.

Powell, Bill, et. al. "Struggle for the Soul of Islam." *Time*, vol. 164, iss. 11. (13 September 2004): 46-64.

Peters, Ralph. "Rolling Back Radical Islam," *Parameters* 32 no. 3 (autumn 2003): 6-9.

Priest, Dana. *The Mission*. New York: W.W. Norton & Co., 2002: 1-40.

Robinson, Linda. "Plan of Attack," *US News & World Report* volume 139, Issue 4 (1 August 2005): 26.

Roswell, Ben and Bathsheba Crocker, *Anti-Americanism in Iraq: An Obstacle to Democracy*. Washington D.C.: Center for Strategic and International Studies, 2004.

Russell, James A. "Strategic Implications of the Iraq Insurgency." *Middle East Review of International Affairs* vol. 8 (Jun 2004): 51.

Sageman, Mark. *Understanding Terror Networks*. PA: Penn Press, 2004: 20.

Sappenfeld, Mark. US Tempers its View of Victory in Iraq." *Chrisitan Science Monitor* (16 September 2005): 1.

Saxton, Jim. "Fighting Terror Four Years on." *Washington Times*. (11 September 2005).

Schwartz, Lowell H. and Jeff Michaels. "Exiting Iraq." *United Press International* (29 August 2005).

Simon, Steven and Jeff Martini. "Terrorism: Denying Al Qaeda its Popular Support," *The Washington Quarterly* vol. 28, Iss. 1 (winter 2004/05): 131-145.

Sisk, Richard. "Military Expert Urges New Plan in Iraq War" *NY Daily News,* (11 September 2005).

Smith, Huston. *Islam: A Concise Introduction.* San Francisco, CA, HarperSanFransico, 2001.

Steiglia, Mark A. *Why they hate us: Disaggregating the Iraqi Insurgency.* Thesis for Naval Postgraduate School, March 2005.

Stern, Jessica. "Preparing for a War on Terrorism" *Current History,* vol.100, iss. 649 (Nov 2001): 355-357.

_____. *Terror in the Name of God: Why Religious Militants Kill.* New York: Harper Collins, 2003.

Tse-Tong, Mao. *On Guerilla Warfare.* Trans. Samuel B. Griffith II. Chicago: University of Illinois Press, 2000.

Tzu, Sun. *The Art of War.* Trans. Samuel B. Griffith. New York: Oxford University Press, 1971.

U.S. Congress. House. Congressional Research Issue brief for Congress by Raphael Perl. "Terrorism and National Security: Issues and Trends." 8 Jun 2005.

U.S. Congress. Senate. Mr. Anthony H. Cordesman, written testimony to U.S. Senate Foreign Relations Committee on United States Strategy in Iraq. 1 February 2005.

U.S. Congress. Senate. LtGen Gregory S. Newbold, USMC (Ret) written testimony to U.S. Senate Foreign Relations Committee on United States Strategy in Iraq. 1 February 2005.

U.S. Congress. Senate. Mr. Peter Khalil written testimony to U.S. Senate Foreign Relations Committee on United States Strategy in Iraq. 1 February 2005.

U.S. Government, *National Strategy for Combating Terrorism*, Washington D.C.: GPO, February 2003.

US Marine Corps. *Small Wars Manual*. (Quantico, VA: United States Marine Corps, 1940).

Voll, Robert Obert. *Islam – Continuity and Change in the Modern World*. New York: Syracuse University Press, 1994: 15-16, 282-310.

Woodward, Bob. *Plan of Attack*. New York: Simon & Schuster, 2004: 8 & 37.

Wolfowitz, Paul. *A Strategic Approach to the Challenge of Terrorism.* (Speech presented to RAND Corporation, Grand Hyatt Washington, Washington D.C. 8 September 2004.)

Zakaria, Fareed. "How to Stop the Contagion." *Newsweek* (1 August 2005*):* 40*.*

_____, "Finally a Smart Iraq Strategy," *Newsweek*, (24 October 2005):33

www.ingramcontent.com/pod-product-compliance
Lightning Source LLC
Chambersburg PA
CBHW080852010626

R18376000001B/R183760PG45790CBX00016B/5